O house
of Ephraim Israel
and house of Judah...
the Father called your name,
a green olive tree, beautiful in fruit
and form. But because of your sins, He
pronounced evil against you. Yet take heart,
O house of Israel, take heart O house of Judah, for
the Father has promised: It will come about that after
I have uprooted and scattered them, after some have become like degenerate, foreign vines, then My compass-
ions will again be kindled and I will regather them. I
will bring them back, each one to his own inheritance,
each one to his own land. Yes, this is My promise to
them. For these two olive branches are My two
chosen witnesses. And I will grant authority to
them, for they are the two sons of fresh oil
who are standing by the LORD
of all the earth.
(Jeremiah
2:18-21;
11:10,16
-17; 12:15;
Hosea 1-2;
Zechariah 4:11-14;
Revelation 11:3-4.)

Special Thanks

Special thanks to Dr. David Cavallaro,
his wife, Gloria (Author, *My Beloved's Israel*),
whose support and encouragement
made this book possible.

The Prophetic Call

The following Scriptures appear on the cover of this book. We list them here along with the reference:

O "House of Israel and House of Judah...YHVH called your name, 'A green olive tree, beautiful in fruit and form'" (Jeremiah 11:10,16). And YHVH says, "Behold, I will take the stick of Joseph, which is in the hand of Ephraim, and the tribes of Israel, his companions; and I will put them with the stick of Judah, and make them one stick...in My hand" (Ezekiel 37:19). "In those days the house of Judah will walk with the house of Israel, and they will come together...to the land I gave their fathers as an inheritance" (Jeremiah 3:18). "It will come about that just as you were a curse among the nations, O house of Judah and house of Israel, so I will save you that you may become a blessing. Do not fear; let your hands be strong" (Zechariah 8:13). "Then the jealousy of Ephraim will depart, and those who harass Judah will be cut off; Ephraim will not be jealous of Judah, and Judah will not harass Ephraim. They will swoop down on the slopes of the Philistines on the west; and YHVH will utterly destroy the tongue of the Sea of Egypt; and He will wave His hand over the River with His scorching wind; and He will strike it into seven streams and make men walk over dry-shod" (Isaiah 11:13-15). "'In those days and at that time,' declares YHVH, 'the sons of Israel will come, both they and the sons of Judah as well; they will go along weeping as they go, and it will be YHVH their God they will seek. They will ask for the way to Zion, turning their faces in its direction; they will come that they may join themselves to YHVH in an everlasting covenant that will not be forgotten" (Jeremiah 50:4-5). "'Behold, days are coming,' declares YHVH, 'when I will make a new covenant with the house of Israel and with the house of Judah, not like the covenant which I made with their fathers in the day I took them by the hand to bring them out of the land of Egypt, My covenant which they broke, although I was a husband to them... But this is the covenant which I will make with the house of Israel after those days...I will put My law within them and on their heart I will write it; and I will be their God, and they shall be My people. They will not teach again, each man his neighbor and each man his brother, saying, "Know YHVH," for they will all know Me, from the least of them to the greatest of them...for I will forgive their iniquity, and their sin I will remember no more" (Jeremiah 31:31-34). "Therefore through this Jacob's iniquity will be forgiven; and this will be the full price of the pardoning of his sin: when he makes all the altar stones like pulverized chalk stones; when Asherim and incense altars will not stand" (Isaiah 27:9). "Return to the stronghold, O prisoners who have the hope; this very day I am declaring that I will restore double to you. For I will bend Judah as My bow, I will fill the bow with Ephraim....and I will make you like a warrior's sword. Then YHVH will appear over them, and His arrow will go forth like lightning; and the Lord YHVH will blow the trumpet, and will march in the storm winds of the south" (Zechariah 9:12-14).

Shema Israel.
Hear and obey the call of the Holy One of Israel.

Contents

Foreword

It is my observation that the GOD of Israel often uses men and women working together to keep His plan for Israel on course. Sometimes He especially chooses to use the female team member. For example, He used Sarah to insure that the promise went to Isaac rather than to Ishmael (the one Abraham would have chosen), and He used Rebekah to thwart Isaac's plan to pass the promise to Esau rather than to Jacob (whom YHVH had chosen) (Genesis 21:9-12; 27:4-10).

I am thankful that the Father has used my wife, Batya, and her faithfulness to help keep our team on course. Because of her tenacity, we can now understand "Israel," and can therefore be used by the Holy One to help accomplish His desire, which is to have a people for His own possession.

In the early Seventies we became deeply involved in the new Messianic Jewish Movement, where we faced two initial challenges. First, we needed to provide a way for Jewish Believers to come to know Y'shua as their Messiah without having to renounce their Jewish heritage. Second, we needed to present Israel's Messiah to the Church from a Jewish perspective, and thus encourage an appreciation for the eternal principles of Torah (the "Law") and for the truths revealed in the Feasts of Israel.

From the beginning, the movement began to attract "Gentiles." In fact, more *non-Jews* were flocking to the standard being raised by Messianic Judaism than were Jewish people. These non-Jews had two motivations: They wanted to support their Jewish brothers, and to trade errant traditions for the Father's Torah and His Feasts. They too were being drawn to this reemerging Israel.

We strongly supported the fledgling efforts of our Jewish brothers. Among other things, we established a real first: The *House of David Messianic Materials Catalogue.*

The goal of this cutting-edge publication was to develop and distribute materials that would aid Believers in understanding both their "roots" and their Jewish brethren.

However, the more we read and observed, the more we became concerned over the place of those regarded as "non-Jews" in the movement. At the time, Messianic Jewish heritage was based on one having "visible" Jewish parentage when they became involved in the movement (or they could simply be married to some-one who met the requirement). These "physical Jews" who accepted Messiah were then assumed to be "spiritual Jews" as well. On the other hand, "Gentiles" who joined the movement were considered to be only "spiritual" heirs, and there was no way for them to attain the Jewish "twice chosen" status.

This standard resulted in two classes of citizenship —which soon caused problems. Many non-Jews were made to feel like second-class citizens. Seeking resolution, I appealed to the leadership to establish a "conversion procedure" that would make everyone equal, both "physically" and "spiritually."

Not only was this proposal unacceptable to most of them, after reflecting on the idea, it became completely unacceptable to my wife. She reasoned that, while all must repent, if one also had to "be converted to be a first-class citizen," then one must have been born wrong in the first place. She would often say, *"A mortal man's declaration will not change the facts of who I am. What I need to know is, Who am I to the Father?"*

The teachings being put forth about the roles of "Israel and the Church" did not seem to be adding up to what we saw in Holy Writ. This fact, plus the challenge of finding Scriptural books about Israel for our Catalogue, led Batya to cry out to the Father with the question, *"Who is Israel?"*

This concise book offers the essence of the Father's answer to that all-important question. Surely the Holy Spirit will use it, along with its parent book, *Who Is Israel?* to help guide a believing Israel back onto the road of "Thy Kingdom come on earth, as it is in heaven." It will help get us back on course, thus preparing the way for Messiah's return and restoration of the Kingdom to Israel.

This brief overview provides answers to the "Israel" question. It shows how Israel was divided into two houses, the house of Ephraim (Israel) and the house of Judah. It emphasizes the fact that our Father is now putting them back together. Additionally, it addresses two other life-changing questions: *Where is Israel now? What is Israel's destiny?*

On a profoundly personal level, this solution driven book will help you answer the following questions: *Who are you to the Father? Why do you feel the way you do about Israel. And what is your individual destiny?*

I believe my wife was called to write the first of our books because in our team she is the "nit-picker" (you need one of those for research purposes). She is never willing to settle for anything less than the absolute truth, regardless of consequences. Furthermore, between the two of us, she is more articulate. But her books speak for both of us. Every word. However, I feel there is another reason that she especially has been called to write on this subject.

I think YHVH wanted this latter-day truth to be presented first by the feminine side of His creation, because in order to reunite a divided Israel, we must all learn to *nurture* one another. We must learn to be patient, to love and encourage each other. In our restoration, we will first have to exhibit an encouraging, mother's type love to those who are "different."

In the Father's grand design, the mothers most often settle squabbles between the children. Very often Ephraim (Israel) and Judah, Christians and Jews, behave like battling, jealous children, and before their age-old disputes can truly be settled, both must be corrected fairly and equitably (Deuteronomy 25:13-16; Proverbs 20:10).

As reunited Israel emerges from their womb of dispersion, they will be like sons who must first learn to heed their "mother's *instructions*" (Proverbs 1:8; 6:20). For Scripture commands us not to "forsake the *torah* of our mother."A Our Mother's torah, or instructions, most often deal with our *heart attitude*s.

A See the *House of David Herald*, Volume Eleven Book Ten, *Mama's Torah*.

Children's training primarily begins with their mothers. Only when a son has matured and developed a right heart attitude is he turned over to his father, who then trains him to become "*bar mitzvah*" (a son of the commandments).

A right heart attitude is necessary to live the Father's Torah. Since women are frequently more intuitive than men, they are generally much better at reaching into the heart of a matter than is fact-oriented man.

To put Israel back together again, we need to become like little children and deal with the issues of our hearts. Moreover, it seems our Father has often used women to get the men moving, and this generation of men needs to have a fire of faithfulness lit under them. There are too many who would rather sit and look for signs than to move out and create wonders.

In the spirit of Deborah of old, Batya issues a call to those who are sitting and waiting like Barak. Hers is an encouraging call to "*Arise, O sons of Israel! Believe that the Father has given your enemies into your hands!*" (Judges 4-5). Her call is a declaration, for the day is upon us when the Holy One of Israel is making the "sticks" of Ephraim and Judah one in His hand (Ezekiel 37:15-28)! Today is the day when *YHVH Tsavaot*, the LORD of Hosts, is calling forth the overcoming armies of Israel!

It has been Sovereignly decreed that Ephraim and Judah ultimately will know victory over their enemies. They will help prepare the way for the return of our King and help establish His Kingdom here on earth (Isaiah 11:11-16). We want to partake of that victory.

Finally, I want to say that the God-given insight

found in our books has brought radical change to my life. It has truly changed me. Further, I have seen this same understanding dramatically change the lives of tens of thousands. And I know it can change you! So I welcome you to the ranks of the radically changed— to the multitude of forerunners being prepared for the day when the kingdoms of this world will become the restored Kingdom of Israel!

Angus Wootten
Director
Messianic Israel Alliance
Saint Cloud, Florida

Introduction

Who is Israel? Our answer to this question is vitally important to each of us; for it determines how we will interpret Scripture and who we think are the Father's "chosen" people, it also defines our view of His end-time plan for His people.

Who are our Heavenly Father's "chosen" people, the "Christians" or the "Jews"? Could the Scriptural answer include both people groups? (Deuteronomy 7:6; 1 Peter 1:1; 2:9).

To answer this critical question we must address the idea of "Physical Israel," for, whether realized or not, a vague concept of physical descent is the usual standard applied when people seek to define whom they think are the people "of Israel." Even those who claim to be "Spiritual Israel" assume they are not of "Physical Israel," and often proclaim that being part of physical Israel is unimportant.

Why is it important for Believers[B] in the Messiah of Israel (Y'shua [C]) to know whether they are part of Israel?

B We use *Believer* to describe those purchased by Messiah's blood rather than *Christian* because the latter is misused (Mat 7:23; 1 Cor 6:20; 1 Pet 1:17-19).
C *Y'shua* (ישוע) is His Hebrew/Aramaic name, it means "Salvation" (Mat 1:21).

The Father says, "Israel is My son, My firstborn" (Exodus 4:22). Conversely, His "firstborn" is "Israel." Israel is a birthright title that is of great importance to the Father. Remember what He said of Esau, who disdained his birthright?

"I have loved Jacob; but I have hated Esau...men will call [Esau]...the people toward whom YHVH[D] is indignant forever" (Malachi 1:2-4).[E] New Covenant Believers are sovereignly warned, "See that no one is ...godless like Esau, who for a single meal sold his inheritance rights as the oldest son." Because, "afterward, as you know, when he wanted to inherit this blessing, he was rejected. He could bring about no change of mind [no place for repentance], though he sought for it with tears" (Hebrews 12:15-17, NIV).

It is crucial that we understand Israel, yet first we must delineate a few salient points:

Israel: Divided By The Almighty

Abraham fathered Isaac, who fathered Jacob (later named Israel), who fathered twelve sons known as the twelve tribes of Israel. After King Solomon's death (son of King David), Israel's tribes were divided into two houses or kingdoms: Ephraim (Israel) and Judah. Solomon's son, Rehoboam, became king of the Southern Kingdom of Judah, and he wanted to force those of the Northern Kingdom (Ephraim/Israel) to come under his rule. However, YHVH warned him, "You shall not go up or fight against your relatives...for this thing is from Me" (2 Chronicles 11:4).

D YHVH: Name of the one true God, comprised of four Hebrew letters, יהוה.
E Gen 25:28-34; Obad 1:6-9,17-18; Jer 49:10; Rom 9:13.

Israel: Not Yet Reunited

Some people teach that the two houses of Israel have already been reunited. However, this cannot be true because the hallmarks of a fully restored Israel are sinlessness, living safely in the Land, and being under the rule of the King of Kings. It is evident that these conditions have not been met; therefore, Israel's two houses could not possibly be fully reunited at this time. As Believers, we realize that Israel's unity is presently imputed in Messiah Y'shua, but Israel has not yet fully implemented that unity (Ezekiel 37:22-26; Isaiah 27:9; Zechariah 8:3,7-8,13; Ephesians 2).

The "Witness People"–Divided Into "Two"

Why did the Father allow division to come to Israel?

"You are My witnesses," He says of Israel's children (Isaiah 43:10). Israelite sheep are always being a "witness," though that witness may be positive or negative, for "the gifts and calling of God are without repentance" (KJV).

Israel is called to witness to the world that YHVH alone is "GOD." She is to proclaim that YHVH is the "I AM," that before Him there was no GOD formed, and that there will be none after Him, and that there is no Savior besides Him (Isaiah 43:8-13; 44:8; Luke 2:11).

But that presents a problem, for, YHVH cannot break His own Law. Moreover, He is the ultimate Author of Israel's Covenants, Old and New. In His Inspired Books He established a law that demands that all things be confirmed by *two or more witnesses...*

Two Houses–Two Witnesses

In Israel two or more must bear witness before a matter can be established, confirmed, or believed. Messiah Y'shua and Paul the apostle upheld this principle. Thus, according to both the Old Covenant and the New Covenant, a matter must first be confirmed by "two or more witnesses." Since YHVH will always abide by His own Torah (or "Law"), He too must have two witnesses to confirm and establish His truth—Genesis to Revelation. F

Historically, for the past nineteen hundred years, YHVH has had two witnesses: Ephraim and Judah, Christians and Jews.

F See Numbers 35:30; Deuteronomy 17:6; 19:15; John 8:17; 2 Corinthians 13:1. Note: This law also reveals the *plurality* of the God of Israel. For He declared that, "No person shall be put to death on the testimony of *one* witness" (Num 35:30; Deu 19:15). In Israel, execution demands, a *plurality* of *witnesses*. And in these verses, *one* is translated from *echad*, which can mean a numeral, united, first, alike, alone, a man, only, other, together, same, single, each (see *Strong's Exhaustive Concordance*, Thomas Nelson, 1984 [also Parson's Technology QuickVerse Bible Software Program, 1996-99, Cedar Rapids], hereafter *Strong's*, # H259; TWOT # 61). *Echad* is used to define our GOD in the *Shema*, the Deuteronomy 6:4 affirmation of faith: "Hear, O Israel...the LORD is one [*echad*]." *Echad* can mean both *alone*—as in *only*, or it can mean *together*—as in *one/united/same*. In the "human witnesses" verses, "echad" must be taken in its "diversity within unity" meaning. And while true that our God is to be the "*One* and *Only* GOD" of the Israelites—it also is true that His *echad* claim must be understood in its "plural" form. For, "Scripture cannot be broken" (John 10:35). And in Scripture YHVH is depicted as a "witness" against the people of Israel (Mal 3:5; Lev 20:5; Deu 32:35; Psa 96:13). Therefore, if He is "singular," and has been a "witness" against a man that leads to the death of that man, then, YHVH Himself has broken Scripture. However, if He is to be a Scripturally correct "witness' against man, then He must be understood in the "diversity within unity" sense of *echad*. The Word does tell us that He is "plural" with Messiah Y'shua—Who ultimately will be both Judge and Jury (John 5:22-24,30-34: 12:48). Y'shua is the Living Word—His Word will one day be used to judge all mankind (John 1:1; Heb 4:12). (See the *House of David Herald*, Vol. 8 Book 9, *One Witness?*, by Batya Wootten and Judith Dennis.)

Though the testimonies of each have thus far been incomplete, they are nevertheless the *only* two people groups on earth who have been giving "testimony" about the God of Abraham, Isaac, and Jacob.

Both Houses: Chosen To Be Tested

Scripture refers to the two houses of Ephraim and Judah as "The two families that YHVH chose." And He swore that He will one day "restore their fortunes and...have mercy on them'" (Jeremiah 33:23-26).

These "two nations" (Ezekiel 35:10; 37:22) also are called "both the houses of Israel" (Isaiah 8:14), and during their sojourn on earth both are called to a "test." We see this in that the word *bachar*, or *chosen*, also is translated *tested*: "Behold, I have refined you, but not as silver; I have tested you in the furnace of affliction" (Isaiah 48:10).

Israel was chosen to forever be "a kingdom of priests and a holy nation." Because YHVH loved their fathers, He *chose*, *bachar* (בחר), or *appointed*, their descendants after them.[G] Because they are *chosen*, Israelites must make a *choice*.

"I call heaven and earth to witness against you today, that I have set before you life and death, the blessing and the curse...so choose life in order that you may live, you and your descendants."

Restated, Israel is forever chosen to choose.

G The *Theological Wordbook of the Old Testament* (hereafter *TWOT*) says of *bachar* (chosen), "The root idea is evidently to 'take a keen look at'...thus... the connotation of 'testing or examining' found in Isa 48:10....The word is [primarily] used to express the choosing which has ultimate and eternal significance" (Moody, 1985, # 231, Vol. I, p 100). See Exo 19:4-6; Deu 4:37; 7:6-8; 10:15; 1 Pet 1:1; 2:9-10. *Chose. Strong's* # H 977.

Israel also is *chosen* to be *tested* (Deuteronomy 30:19; 28). So choose this day whom you will serve O Israel (Joshua 24:15).

Ephraim Israel:
Destined To Become A *Melo haGoyim*

To understand Israel we must realize that whether they are blessed or cursed, Israelites and their children will forever remain biological Israelites. Further, just as every promise made to the Jewish people must be fulfilled, so every promise made to Judah's brother Joseph, and thus to Joseph's son Ephraim, must be fulfilled. Jacob proclaimed that the descendants of Ephraim would become a "*melo hagoyim*" (מלא הגוים), a "fullness of Gentiles" (Genesis 48:19).

Where is Ephraim today?

Could he possibly be among the non-Jewish Believers? Could the roots of many Believers extend much deeper than previously imagined? Is it possible that at this time the Father is revealing the truth of Ephraim's identity as "part" of the people of Israel?

Certainly that would explain why so many Believers now feel drawn to Israel's feasts and to the eternal truths of Torah. It also explains Jeremiah's prophecy about Ephraim being "instructed," and about him "coming to know himself." It well explains Ephraim's present search for his roots (Jeremiah 31:18-19).

As foretold by Isaiah, both houses have stumbled over He Who would be a Sanctuary to them (Y'shua)—although they stumbled in different ways. Judah has stumbled in not seeing the Messiah as the Living Torah, Ephraim has stumbled in that he could not see the truth of his own Israelite roots. This happened because both were partially hardened. Neither could see clearly. But now is the time for the veil to be lifted and for blinded eyes to begin to see. It is time for the "two sticks" of Ephraim and Judah to be made one in the Father's hand (Isaiah 8:13-14; John 2:19-22; Romans 11:25; Ezekiel 37:15-28).

This Restoration Includes "All"

Israel's full restoration includes *all* who are called in Messiah. It includes those who were at one time "separate from Messiah, excluded from the commonwealth of Israel, and strangers to the covenants of promise, having no hope and without God in the world." In Y'shua, those who formerly were far off are brought near by His shed blood. "So then you are no longer strangers and aliens, but you are fellow citizens with the saints, and are of God's household" (Ephesians 2:11-22). This Divine restoration includes the "companions" of both Judah and Ephraim (Ezekiel 37:16).

Israelites, Ephraimites and Judahites alike, are beginning to see truths in Scripture that they never saw before, because their eyes are being opened.[H]

This new insight is causing Israel to come forth from her grave of disobedience and dispersion, and to leave behind her tattered shrouds of Roman *and* Babylonian garb. It is causing her to seek to be clothed only in truth and righteousness. She is returning to the Father's Inspired Word, Genesis to Revelation, and in her search for truth, Scripture is coming alive with new meaning.

H Jer 11:10, 16; 2:18,21; Rom 11:25; Isa 8:14; Gen 48:19.

Though people often make it complicated, the truth about the identity of Israel is very simple:

Long ago the Father divided Israel into two houses: Ephraim (Israel) and Judah. As His "two witnesses" they were sent in two different directions to serve two different purposes, to establish His two immutable truths of Law and Grace. And now, in this last day, YHVH would have the two Israel's come together, that they might fulfill His Divine purpose and begin to confirm His truth in the earth.

That is the simple essence of this book. So as you go through the confirming verses in this condensed overview, please remember the simplicity behind it all:

Two houses—Two directions—Two different purposes—Now it is time to put them back together again.

My prayer is that as you study the Father's Word concerning Israel, that He will enlighten the eyes of your heart and keep you from every deception and error of man. May you come to know His plan for your life, may He give you the boldness to courageously walk in that great plan. May it be that you hear His voice alone, as He quietly whispers in your ear, "This is the way, walk ye in it" (Ephesians 1:18; Jeremiah 29:11; Isaiah 30:21).

Shalom b' Y'shua,
Batya

One

Many Israels—One Israel

Where do we look to see Israel in all its glory? Though there are many Christians and Jews who live exemplary lives, to truly see and understand Israel, we must first come to know the most important Israel of all.

Following the Father's call of Jacob, for two thousand years the twelve tribes of Israel appeared to be Jacob's heirs—even though they were divided into two houses. Then in Israel a Son was born. He often called Himself "the Son of Man" (Daniel 7:13; Matthew 12:8; 12:40). The life and death of this Son of Man served to divide Israel once again. It is a conflict that has continued for more than 1900 years. Today two people groups—many adherents of Christianity and virtually all followers of Judaism— lay claim to the coveted title of "Israel." Each group claims to be the true heirs of the patriarchs. Most deny the other group the right to the title. What is the truth? Who *is* Israel?

First and foremost, Israel is depicted in Messiah Y'shua. He is the epitome of all that Israel is called to be. Nonetheless, the most common responses to the "Israel" question are—

- ♈ Jacob, Whose Name Was Changed to Israel
- ♈ The Sons of Jacob—The Twelve Tribes
- ♈ The Land Given to the Twelve Tribes
- ♈ The Old-Covenant People of the God of Israel
- ♈ The Ten Tribes of the Northern Kingdom
- ♈ The Church
- ♈ The Jewish People
- ♈ The Present Jewish State

However, let us remember that Messiah Y'shua also is named Israel. In Isaiah both the Father and Y'shua speak: "Listen to Me, O islands [the nations].... From the body of My mother He named Me [says Y'shua]. And He has made My mouth like a sharp sword....And He said to Me, 'You are My Servant, Israel, in Whom I will show My glory'.... And now says YHVH who formed Me from the womb to be His Servant, to bring Jacob back to Him, in order that Israel might be gathered to Him...To raise up the tribes of Jacob and to restore the preserved ones of Israel; I will also make You [Y'shua] a light of the nations so that My salvation [Y'shua] may reach to the end of the earth" (Isaiah 49:1-6).

Y'shua fulfills the above prophecy in many ways:

It was said to Mary/Miriam: "She will bear a Son; and...call His name Y'shua, for He will save His people from their sins." YHVH calls Y'shua, "My Servant Whom I have chosen." Y'shua says, "I will make war against them with the sword of My mouth." Also, Y'shua is "the radiance of His [YHVH's] glory and the exact representation of His nature." And He is, "A light of revelation to the Gentiles, and the glory of...Israel" (Matthew 1:21; 12:18; Revelation 2:16; Hebrews 1:3; Luke 2:32; 1:3).

The Father says, "Israel is My son, My firstborn,"

and "Out of Egypt I called My son." Matthew says: "So was fulfilled what YHVH said through the prophet: 'Out of Egypt I called My son'" (Exodus 4:22; Hosea 11:1; Matthew 2:15).

YHVH says of Y'shua, "I will appoint you...as a light to the nations, to open blind eyes, to bring out prisoners." And, "The people who walk in darkness will see a great light."[1] Y'shua came "to fulfill what was spoken through Isaiah the prophet: The land of Zebulun and the land of Naphtali, by the way of the sea, beyond the Jordan, Galilee of the Gentiles [former Ephraimite territories]—The people who were sitting in darkness saw a great light, to those who were sitting in the...shadow of death, upon them a light dawned" (Isaiah 42:6-7; 9:2; Matthew 4:14-16). Further, Y'shua said, "I am the light of the world." And YHVH gave Him "the throne of His father David," that He might "reign over the house of Jacob forever" in a kingdom without end [2] (John 8:12; 9:5; Luke 1:32-33).

YHVH is "summing up all things in Y'shua" (NASB); He is gathering "together in one all things" (KJV); He is bringing "all things in heaven and on earth...under one head, even Christ" (NIV). He is the appointed "heir of all things" (Ephesians 1:10; Hebrews 1:2). This "summation" includes Israel. Y'shua is the Israel who is gathering scattered Jacob. To see Israel summed up in all its Glory, we first must look to her Messiah, Y'shua.

---

1 Hosea 8:8; Amos 9:9; Isa 8:14; Rom 11:11,25.
2 When Y'shua "made purification of sins, He sat down at the right hand of the Majesty on high." He now sits on the throne of His father David and rules over the house of Jacob. His Kingdom is now and yet to come (Exo 19:6; 2 Sam 7:12-16; Luke 1:32-33; 12:32; Dan 7:22; Rev 5:9-10; 20:6:1 Peter 1:1; 2:5-10; Heb 1:3; 8:1; 3:6; 10:19). He offers a new covenant that is both now and yet to come. Only when we are no longer teaching our neighbor about YHVH (because we all know Him) have we entered into its fullness (Jer 31:31-33; Heb 8:8-12).

Both Houses Have Misunderstood Y'shua

Blinded Ephraim has misunderstood Y'shua in certain ways. Some think He did away with the "law," because they misunderstand His statement, "Do not think that I came to abolish the Law or the Prophets; I did not come to abolish but to fulfill" (Matthew 5:17).

Some laws cannot be eliminated. Gravity is an example. It is a law that we have to recognize, because if we break the law of gravity we may die. Similarly, if we break the eternal Instructions of Torah we will suffer consequences. This is not because our Heavenly Father waits eagerly to catch us in transgressions, but because His laws have automatic results. It is the principal of sowing and reaping. For example, if we do not take a Sabbath rest every seventh day, we risk having our bodies break down due to stress. Our Heavenly Father wants us to have a day in which we can take our focus from the things of the world and turn to Him, to His love, and to His provision. Thus we find both earthly and Heavenly rest in Him.

Did Y'shua Do Away With The Law?

Yes and no. Yes, because as our sacrificial lamb, Y'shua was offered once for all, and we no longer "need daily... sacrifices" (Hebrews 7:27; 9:12; 10:10; 1 Peter 3:18; Jude 1:3; 1 Corinthians 5:7). No, because the laws of Torah continue to be wisdom to us. They make us a stronger, healthier, wiser people when we reverence them: "You shall therefore keep every commandment...so that you may be <u>strong</u> and go in and possess the land [and]...<u>prolong</u> your days" (Deuteronomy 11:8-9).

Torah—Letter or Love?

Y'shua said, "If you love Me, you will keep My commandments" (John 14:15). In this vein of love, He fulfilled the Law. He walked it out in all its glory, for our God is a God of love. His Torah (or instructions) were given to help us succeed. His Torah is the constitution of our Nation. It is the history of our forefathers. In the pages of Torah we find understanding. It outlines a blessed path that keeps us from shame (1 John 4:8; 1 Kings 2:3; Deuteronomy 4:5-6; Psalm 119:1-6).

On the other hand, if we focus on the letter of the law, if we seek eternal salvation through the keeping of these laws, then we shall surely fail. We shall be found wanting, for Israel must focus on the "spirit" of Torah.

We must allow Ruach haKodesh (the Holy Spirit) to write the Father's precious truths on our hearts (Jeremiah 31:31-33; Hebrews 8:10; 10:16).

Torah must first be rooted in nurturing love, like that of a mother. Proverbs instructs us to listen to, and not to forsake the Torah of our mothers (Proverbs 1:8 and 6:20). [3] Mothers deal with heart attitudes, and true Torah can only be presented with a right attitude of heart, as Y'shua demonstrated.

The Redeemer

While Ephraim needs to learn to revere the truths of Torah, and to no more regard its precepts as a "strange thing" (Hosea 8:12), Judah needs to see the truth about Y'shua.

---

3 See the *House of David Herald*, Volume Eleven Book Ten, *Mama's Torah*.

All Israel needs to be redeemed, and only a Divine Elohim/God can redeem our souls from sheol and provide eternal redemption (Psalm 49:10,15).

If we compromise Y'shua's identity as Elohim, Israel loses her Redeemer. And Ephraim often gets tripped up in man-made legalisms as he is drawn to return to Torah and to Israel's feasts. Because he is jealous of Judah and his roots (Isaiah 11:13), Ephraim seeks Judah's approval. But Judah has been hardened to the truth of Messiah's Deity, and so resists the very idea of a divine Redeemer.

Redeemed Israel must avoid this pitfall. We must walk in the eternal truths of Torah while holding tightly to the hand of our Divine Redeemer.

There is much work to be done to bring all Israel into her fullness—but in and through Y'shua it can be done and it will be done. To reunite Israel we look to the epitome of Israel. We look to Y'shua for eternal redemption and for portrayal of a Torah-based walk.

When we walk as He walked, the world will in truth see *Israel*.

Two

Israel Revealed

The following is a succinct collection of writings, graphics, maps and charts (see *Maps and Charts* section) that will help you to see and understand Israel's reemerging two houses, as well as YHVH's latter-day plan for their restoration. We invite you to look up and study the Scripture verses, asking the Holy Spirit, the *Ruach HaKodesh*, to guide you in all truth. For a thorough study of Israel, we invite you to read the comprehensive book, *Who Is Israel?*

- ♦ Abraham was promised myriads of physical descendants (Gen 12:3; 15:1-6; 17:1-6; Rom 4:19-22).

- ♦ Abraham's blessing cannot be separated from that of Isaac and Jacob, because the three were joint heirs (Gen 26:3; 28:4; 1 Chr 16:16-17; Heb 11:9,39-40).

- ♦ Abraham's blessing of multiplicity was given to Isaac, to Jacob, to Joseph, and then to Ephraim (Gen 12:3; 15:5; 17:4; 26:4; 24:24,60; 28:3,14; 32:12; 48:4,16,19).

- Ephraim was declared to be Jacob/Israel's firstborn heir (Deu 21:17; Gen 48:1-22; 1 Chr 5:1-2; Ezek 37:19).

- Ephraim's seed was destined to become a *melo hagoyim*, a fullness of Gentiles (Gen 48:19; Rom 11:25; Isa 8:14 [*melo.* see Psa 24:1]).

- Israel was divided into two houses, into Northern and Southern Kingdoms, which were known as Israel (Ephraim)   and Judah (1 Ki 11:11-13, 26,31-35; 12:15,24; 2 Chr 11:4; Isa 8:14).

- Israel is a "firstborn" title. The firstborn is to be given a double portion that he might be enabled to act as redeemer to his brethren. This title was passed to Ephraim because he became Jacob's firstborn heir (Deu 21:17 25:5-9; Exo 4:22; Jer 31:9; Ruth 3:9; Isa. 59:20; 61:7; Gen 48:22; 1 Chr 5:1-2; Ezek 37:18).

- Ephraim was sent into captivity in Assyria (around 722 BC) and Judah into Babylon (around 586 BC). Many have viewed their captivities as one, but there were many years and many miles of difference between them (2 Ki 17:6,24; 1 Chr 5:26; Ezek 1:1; 1 Ki 14:15).

- Ephraim became "LoAmi" (Not A People) and was swallowed up among the nations. They were therefore lost to their Israelite identity (Hosea 1:10; 2:1,21-23; 8:8; Rom 9:23; Amos 9:9).

- Israel is forever Chosen to Choose: All Israelites and their seed must choose either to follow and obey the Holy One of Israel or to follow other gods (Deu 28:1-68; 30:19; Josh 24:15).

♦ The facts about our biological heritage cannot be changed based on our faith or lack of faith. Israelites are forever biological Israelites. Furthermore, there is an eternal call on all of Israel's seed (Deu 4:37; 7:6-8; 10:15; Exo 19:4-6; Jer 31:37; 33:25-26; Rom 11:28-29).

♦ Though scattered among the nations,, lost Ephraimites continue to be physical Israelites, just as Judahites continue to be physical Jews (Jer 31:20; 2 Ki 17:23; Zech 11:14; Dan 9:7; 1 Chr 5:26; Eph 2:17.Hosea 5:3; 8:8; Amos 9:9; Deu 28:64).

♦ Ephraim has been "lost" to, and thus is ignorant of, his Israelite heritage (Hosea 1-2; 4:1,6: Jer 31:18-19).

♦ The prophet Ezra spoke of a sacrifice given for "all Israel," which in this case defines *only those present*. This verse does not prove that *all biological Israelites* were present. Just as the Jewish people who remained in Babylon continued to be Jews, so the Ephraimites not present (which was the great majority of them) continued to be lost tribes (Ezra 8:25; 1 Ki 12:20 [for another limited use of the word, "all," see 1 Sam 18:16]).

♦ Reunited Israel will be sinless, will not be uprooted from the Promised Land, and Y'shua will reign over them (Isa 11:11-14; Jer 3:14-18; 16:11-16; 50:4-5,20; Zech 8:3,7,13; 9:13; 10:7,8,10; Hos 11:10; Obad 1:18; 1 Sam 17:45; Ezek 37:22-26; Isa 27:9).

♦ Ephraim and Judah are YHVH's two chosen families (Jer 33:23-26; Ezek 35:10; 37:22; Isa 8:14; Zech 2:12; 1 Pet 1:1; 2:9).

♦ The chosen people of Israel are YHVH's witnesses (Isa 43:8-13; 44:8; Num 35:30; Deu 17:6; 19:15; John 8:17; 10:35; 2 Cor 13:1).

♦ YHVH divided His witness people into two houses (2 Chr 11:4; Isa 43:10; Num 35:30; Deu 17:6; 19:15; John 8:17; 2 Cor 13:1; Num 13:2,6,8; Rev 11:3,4; 1:20 Zech 4:11,14).

♦ Messiah Y'shua is also named Israel, and is gathering the scattered seed of Jacob/Israel (Isa 49:1-6; 42:6-7; 9:2; Matt 1:18-,21; 2:15; 4:14-16; Rev 2:16; Ezek 34:10; John 10:11; Luke 2:32).

♦ Y'shua made a New Covenant with the sons of Israel seated at His New Covenant Passover table (Jer 31:31-33; Luke 22:20; Heb 8:6-12; 1 Cor 5:7).

♦ Y'shua has one flock. He is one with the Father. Together they have one people. With earthly Israel, people can be in various stages of "acceptability" to the Father, meaning Israelites can be blessed or cursed and still be "Israelites" (John 10:16,27-30; 17:11,20-21; Matt 2:6; 15:24; 1 John 5:8; Ezek 34; Deu 28).

♦ In ancient Israel foreigners joined Israel by observing circumcision, Passover, and sojourning. The Father made it a perpetual statute that they were thereafter to be regarded as natives of the Land (Lev 19:34; Num 9:14; 15:15,16; Deut 18:15-19; Isa 56:3,6-8; Ezek 47:23).

♦ Israel's three citizenship rules were continued in New Covenant Israel as: 1) circumcision of heart; 2) Y'shua's Passover of Bread and Wine; 3) living in harmony with those of His Kingdom (Matt 21:43; Luke 12:32; 22:30; Dan 7:9-22; Acts 1:6; 1 Pet 1:1; 2:9; Heb 7:12; John 1:29; 1 Cor 5:7; Rev 3:20; Jer 4:4; Heb 7:27; 9:12; 10:10; Acts 15:21; Jer 31:33; Eph 2:12-19).

♦ In the New Covenant, non-Jewish Believers are said to be "former Gentiles." Once they come to faith in the Messiah of Israel they are no longer heathens, but are instead called to begin walking as Israelites, and are part of that commonwealth (Eph 2:11-22.Matt 18:17; 5:47; 6:7; 2 Cor 6:17; 1 Thes 4:5; 1 Pet 2:12).

♦ The *church/ekklesia/congregation* was said to be in the wilderness, and it was thought by the Early Believers to be one with Israel. Thus, the true *church/ekklesia/ congregation* cannot be "separate from Israel," as is often taught (Acts 7:38; Heb 4:2).

♦ Believers belong to Y'shua's *ekklesia/congregation* of the firstborn (Heb 12:22-23).

♦ The word "adoption" is used only five times in Scripture. All of the verses speak of Believers becoming sons of God (Abraham is not even mentioned). All who would be YHVH's sons —Jew and non-Jew alike—must receive this spirit of adoption, which is specifically said to "belong to the sons of Israel" (Rom 8:15,16,23; 9:4; Gal 4:5; Eph 1:5).

♦ True worshipers must worship in spirit and truth. This means all physical Israelites are called to be spiritual, and all spiritual people are physical because they descend from someone. If there is such a thing as "spiritual Israel," then whom are they descended from? Abraham was promised "myriads" of physical descendants, so could not many of the "spiritual" Believers in Messiah actually be physical descendants of Abraham? Moreover, how can one prove they are _not_ descended from him? (John 4:23; Gen 12:3; 15:1-6; 17:1-6).

♦ The olive tree of Israel had two major branches, Ephraim and Judah. The Root, or Life-source, of the tree is Y'shua. Even the patriarchs must be rooted in Him (Jer 11:10,16; 2:18,21; Rom 11:25; Isa 8:13-14; Rev 22:16; Rom 3:23).

♦ Believers in Messiah Y'shua are not to be arrogant toward the Jewish branches that were broken off for unbelief in Him. Instead, they are to lovingly provoke Judah to jealousy, that they might be grafted into the tree again (Obad 1:12; Joel 2:32-3:1; Luke 13:1-5; Rom 11:11,18-21).

♦ Ephraim is jealous of Judah and his roots. Judah vexes Ephraim by refusing to recognize him as an equal heir in Israel. To end their ancient quarrel, Ephraim first needs to change, and to cause Judah to see something in Ephraim that he wants (Isa 11:13).

♦ Ephraim will repent of his youthful sins when instructed about his own Israelite roots, when he comes to know himself and understands that he too is part of Israel. He also needs to realize that Judah is his brother and to begin to treat his as such (Jer 31:18,19).

♦ Ephraim is called to be a watchman for the whole house of Israel (Hosea 9:8; Jer 31:6; 30:24; Isa 48:6; Hab 2:1).

♦ Ephraim is destined to return to the Land in righteousness, in might, and in power (Jer 31:21; Ezek 37:23; Hos 1:10; Zec 10:7).

♦ The first example of two witnesses who gave a good report about the God of Israel were Caleb and Joshua—a Judahite and an Ephraimite (Num 13:2,6,8).

♦ Y'shua gives His two witnesses the power to prophesy, and He describes them as two olive trees and "two lampstands." Lampstands are *ekklesias*/congregations. In the last days, Y'shua calls forth two "congregations" of peoples. (In addition, there may well be two "individual witnesses"—men who will possibly will lead the two reunited houses in the war against the Beast). (Rev 1:20; 11:3,4; 16:3-4; 11-20).

♦ Zechariah says the two olive trees are anointed to serve the LORD of all the earth (Zech 4:11,14).

♦ YHVH is now calling forth two congregations of peoples—Judah and Ephraim. He is making these two sticks (or trees) as one in His hand. Moreover, books are made from trees, and the two Books of Old and New Covenants need to be affirmed by the two witnesses, Judah and Ephraim, as being "one" Book of Covenants (Ezek 37:15-28).

♦ Our Father declared a latter-day plan to reunite the two houses: both will come to repentance and both will be joined to one another in power (Deu 33:7; Micah 5:3; Zech 8:23; Jer 3:17-18; 50:4; Daniel 7:27; Hosea 11:8-10; Amos 9:11; Luke 12:32; Rom 11; Isa 27:9).

♦ Judah will believe in Messiah when he sees Ephraim, or a reunited Israel, properly representing both the Messiah and YHVH's Torah. Judah has been blind to the Messiah and Ephraim has been blind to the truths of Torah, yet now both must begin to see. Those in the Olive Tree must work to help make this truth a reality (Matt 23:37-39; Rom 11; Isa 8:14).

♦ When Ephraim and Judah are united in YHVH Elohim, when their reunion is fully manifested, and when they become like their Messiah, loving not their lives even unto death, then they will become a sinless, invincible army. When they are ready to lay down their lives for their faith, then they will be sovereignly empowered to fight the battles of the GOD of Israel (Isa 11:14; Zech 9:13-10:10; 13:2; Hosea 1:11; Amos 9:10; Zeph 3:11-13).

♦ *Shema Yisrael... Hear and obey O Israel.* (Gen 49:2; Deu 6:4; Hos 5:1; Ezek 36:1).

Three

Ten Tips To Help You Understand Israel

Study the following Scriptures and the Word will come alive with new personal meaning.

1) Like the United States, Israel was once divided into Northern and Southern Kingdoms—and they have never been fully reunited (Jer 3:14-18; Isa 11:14; Zech 8:3-13; 10:7-10; Ezek 37:15-28).

2) Scripture calls these two kingdoms, "both the houses of Israel," "YHVH's "two nations," and "the two families that YHVH chose" (Isa 8:14; Ezek 35:10; 37:22; Jer 33:23-26).

3) Those of Ephraim, the Northern Kingdom of Israel, were scattered among every nation. There they were destined to become a "*melo hagoyim*," a "fullness of Gentiles" (Hosea 1-2; 8:8; Amos 9:9; Rom 11).

4) The gifts and calling of the GOD of Israel are without repentance. Therefore there remains an eternal call on all Israel, both Judah and Ephraim, to love and obey Him (Deu 28:1-6; Num 23: 19; Isa 43:10; Rom 11:29).

5) The Ephraimites became degenerate, wild, olive

branches. However, once they have returned to the Olive Tree of Israel, they are called to walk in such a way that will provoke those of Judah to be jealous of them and to want what they have (Jer 11: 10,16; 2:18, 21; Rom 11; 9:26; Hosea 1:9,1; Isa 35:10; Ezek 37:16).

6) Non-Jewish Believers in Messiah are heirs of Abraham's promise, and therefore share citizenship in the commonwealth of Israel (Gen 17:4-7; Rom 4:17; Gal 3:29; Eph 2:11-22).

7) When the Father makes the "two sticks" of Ezekiel "one stick in His hand" Israel will no longer be plucked up from the Land, will no longer defile themselves with any of their transgressions, and will have one king—the King of Kings and Lord of Lords. A fully reunited Israel is a sinless Israel that lives under Messiah's rule in the Land of Promise (Ezek 37:15-28).

8) It is the Father's perpetual statute that a foreigner will be regarded as a native of the Land, and no longer a gentile or heathen, once he has fulfilled the three proscribed rules of Passover, circumcision, and sojourning (Exo 12:48; Lev 19:34; Num 9: 14; Isa 56:3; Eph 2:11-19).

9) Jews and Christians—Judah and Ephraim— are called to serve as two witnesses for the God of Israel. Their divine purpose is to confirm the truth of His Word, from Genesis to Revelation, in all the earth (Num 35:30; Deu 17:6; 19:15; John 8:17; 2 Cor 13:1).

10) Israel was to be a "mystery" until the "fullness of Gentiles," the "*melo hagoyim*" promised to Ephraim "be come in." The veil is being lifted in these last days, and all Israel is coming to understand the formerly hidden truth about the partial hardening of both the houses of Israel—Judah and Ephraim (Rom 11:25; Gen 48:19; Jer 31:18,19).

Four

A List, Key Verses, FAQ's and Prayers

YHVH is dealing with *two* houses of Israel. He has:

- ♦ Two Houses (Isa 8:14; Jer 31:31-33; Heb 8:8-10)
- ♦ Two Nations (Ezek 35:10)
- ♦ Two Chosen Families (Jer 33:24)
- ♦ Two Sisters (Ezek 23:2-4)
- ♦ Two Olive Branches (Zech 4:11-14; Jer 11:10, 16-17; 2:18,21; Rom 11; Rev 11:4)
- ♦ Two Sticks (Ezek 37:15-28)
- ♦ Two Witnesses (Rev 11:3-4)
- ♦ Two Lampstands (Rev 11:3-4)
- ♦ Two Silver Trumpets (Num 10:2-3)
- ♦ Two Leavened Loaves (Heb 9:28)
- ♦ Two Cherubim (Exo 25:18-20)
- ♦ Two Armies That Dance (Song of Song 6:4,13)

To understand Israel, we must realize that the Father has been dealing with **_two_** houses of Israel, Judah and Ephraim, and He now wants us to become **_one_** stick in His hand (Ezek 37:15-28).

Key Verses To Remember

To help you understand and share your faith about both the houses of Israel, you may want to cross-reference some affirming Scriptures in your Bibles. For example, next to Genesis 48:19, write in Psalm 24:1 and Romans 11:25. At Romans 11:25 write in Genesis 48:19 and Psalm 24:1, and so on. In this way, if you remember only one of the verses related to the subject, you can pick up the trail that leads to the other confirming verses.

Ephraim Was To Become A Melo haGoyim:

Ephraim was destined to become a "fullness [*melo*] of Gentiles." Psalm 24:1 also uses "fullness [*melo*]" and thus helps define the word, which speaks of vast numbers of biological heirs from Ephraim. Romans Eleven explains that a partial hardening has happened to Israel (both houses) and that this hardening, this inability to see, was to last until "the fullness of Gentiles" was come in. In other words, we could not see the fullness of this truth until now.

"But...[Jacob] refused and said, 'I know, my son... he [Ephraim] also will become a people and he also will be great. However, his younger brother shall be greater than he, and his descendants shall become a [*melo hagoyim*] fullness of the nations'" (Genesis 48:19).

"The earth is YHVH's, and the [*melo*] fullness thereof" (Psalms 24:1, KJV).

"For I do not want you, brethren, to be uninformed of this mystery—so that you will not be wise in your own estimation—that a partial hardening has happened to Israel until the fullness of the Gentiles has come in" (Romans 11:25).

The Two "Stumbling" Houses of Israel

Both the houses of Israel were destined to stumble over the Sanctuary, Who is Messiah Y'shua. Thus, <u>after</u> the time of Y'shua, there had to be two houses of Israel, both of which would stumble over Him. They would stumble because both were Israel, and "Israel" was hardened and blinded, although in different ways. John reveals that the "Sanctuary" is Y'shua, and that His disciples believed "the Scripture"—which speaks of Isaiah 8:14. Romans 11 reveals that Israel stumbled because they were hardened.

"...<u>YHVH of hosts...shall become a sanctuary</u>; but to both the houses of Israel, a stone to strike and a rock to <u>stumble</u> over..." (Isaiah 8:13-14).

Y'shua said, "Destroy this <u>temple</u>, and in three days I will raise it up.' The Jews then said, 'It took forty-six years to build this temple, and will You raise it up in three days?' But He was speaking of the temple of His body. So when He was raised from the dead, His disciples remembered that He said this; and they believed <u>the Scripture</u> [Isaiah 8:14] and the word which Y'shua had spoken" (John 2:19-22).

"For I do not want you, brethren, to be uninformed of this mystery—so that you will not be wise in your own estimation—that <u>a partial hardening</u> has happened to Israel [both houses] until the fullness of the Gentiles [see Genesis 48:19] has come in" (Romans 11:25).

The Patriarchs and Myriads of Physical Heirs

Abraham, Isaac, and Jacob were promised myriads of physical descendants. The essence of this blessing of multiplicity was passed to Joseph's son, Ephraim. If we have the "faith of Abraham," we too will believe that myriads of descendants sprang from his loins, and that they were to become a "great congregation of peoples." This is not to say that all Believers *must* be physical heirs, but to emphasize that myriads of physical heirs were promised to Abraham. Only the Father in Heaven knows the actual number of biological descendants. We cannot prove that we *are*, or *are not*, biological descendants of Abraham.

"After these things the word of the LORD came to Abram in a vision, saying, 'Do not fear, Abram, I am a shield to you; Your reward shall be very great.' Abram said, 'O Lord GOD, what will You give me, since I am childless, and the heir of my house is Eliezer of Damascus?' And Abram said, 'Since You have given no offspring to me, one born in my house is my heir.' Then behold, the word of the LORD came to him, saying, 'This man will not be your heir; but <u>one who will come forth from your own body, he shall be your heir</u>.' And He took him outside and said, 'Now look toward the heavens, and <u>count the stars</u>, if you are able to count them.' And He said to him, '<u>So shall your descendants be</u>.' Then he believed in the LORD; and He reckoned it to him as righteousness" (Genesis 15:1-6).

The Holy One also said to him "'I am the Almighty God, walk before Me and be blameless. And I will establish My covenant between Me and you, and I will multiply you <u>exceedingly</u>.' And Abram fell on his face, and God talked with him, saying, 'Behold, My covenant is with you, and you will be the father of a <u>multitude of nations</u>. No longer shall your name be called Abram, or "exalted father," but your name shall be Abraham, "father of a multitude." For I will make you the father of a multitude of nations.[4] I will make you <u>exceedingly fruitful</u>, I will make <u>nations</u> of you'" (Genesis 17:1-6).

The New Covenant says of Abraham, "Without becoming weak in faith <u>he contemplated his own body</u>, now as good as dead since he was about a hundred years old, and the deadness of Sarah's womb; yet, with respect to the promise of God, he did not waver in unbelief, but grew strong in faith, giving glory to God, and being fully assured that what He had promised, He was able also to perform. Therefore, 'It was reckoned to him as righteousness'" (Romans 4:19-22).

YHVH said He would make the "fewest of all peoples....as numerous as the stars of the sky" (Deuteronomy 7:7; Exodus 32:13). (By not seeing this truth, have we missed the miracle of His sovereign multiplication of Abraham's seed?)

YHVH's promised Isaac, "I will <u>multiply</u> [5] your descendants <u>as the stars of heaven</u>" (Genesis 26:4).

The blessing given Isaac's wife, Rebekah, was, "Be the mother of <u>thousands of millions</u>," or, "<u>myriads</u>" (Genesis 24:60).[6]

---

4 Abraham believed he would father a multitude of nations, *hamon goyim* (המון גוים). *Strong's* says *Goyim* (גוים), the Hebrew word for Gentiles/Nations (# H1471) means, "a foreign nation...heathen...people." *The New Brown-Driver-Briggs-Gesenius Hebrew-Aramaic Lexicon* (hereafter: *BDBL*) says *goyim* means "nation, people," and is "usually [used to speak] of non-Hebrew people" (#H1471; Hendrickson, 1979; Parsons Technology, 1999). The *Theological Wordbook of the Old Testament* 2 Vol., Moody, 1981, says, "goyim...usually refers to..the surrounding pagan nations" (# 326e).

5 Multiply, *rabah* (רבה), to increase, exceedingly, become numerous, great. *Strong's* and *BDBL* # H 7235; *TWOT* # 2103, 2104.

6 *Strong's* and *BDBL* #'s H 505 and 7235.

Together, they passed their multitudinous blessing to their son Jacob: "May God...make you fruitful and multiply you, that you may become a <u>congregation of peoples</u>" [7] (Genesis 28:3).

The Father promised Jacob, "<u>Thy seed shall be as the dust of the earth</u>, and thou shalt spread abroad to the west, and to the east, and to the north, and to the south" (Genesis 28:14, KJV).

Separating the Blessing of the Patriarchs
Separating the "Ekklesia" From Israel:

Some people try to separate the blessing of Abraham from that of Isaac and Jacob, claiming that non-Jews are "spiritual heirs" of Abraham, but are not heirs of Isaac and Jacob. However, Abraham's blessing cannot be separated from that of Isaac and Jacob, because the three were joint heirs. Moreover, many try to separate the true *ekklesia* (or church) from Biblical Israel. Yet neither of these positions are Scriptural concepts:

YHVH said to Isaac, "To you and to your seed...I will establish <u>the oath which I swore to your father Abraham</u>" (Genesis 26:3).

Isaac said to Jacob, "May He [YHVH] also <u>give you the blessing of Abraham</u>" (Genesis 28:4).

"The covenant which He [God] made with Abraham, and His oath to Isaac, He also <u>confirmed to</u>

---

7 From Jacob YHVH would call forth a *congregation*—a *kahal* (קהל). This Hebrew word is primarily translated *congregation* and is especially used to describe an assembly, company, congregation, or convocation, called together by the Almighty for religious purposes. See *TWOT* # 1991a; also *Strong's* and *BDBL* # H 6951.

Jacob for a statute, to Israel as an everlasting covenant" (1 Chronicles 16:16-17).

Abraham "lived as an alien in the land of promise...with Isaac and Jacob, fellow heirs of the same promise" (Hebrews 11:9).

"These were all commended for their faith, yet none of them received what had been promised...only together with us [New Covenant Believers [8]] would they be made perfect" (Hebrews 11:39-40, NIV).

In the *Brit Chadashah* (New Covenant), ancient Israel is called "the *ekklesia* [congregation] that was in the wilderness" (Acts 7:38).

And, Y'shua used *ekklesia*, the word usually translated (or mistranslated) "church," [9] to describe the assembly He would build (Matthew 16:18, 18:17).

We conclude that both Y'shua and the First Century Believers knew that Israel, the *kahal* [10] and

---

8 "The prophets...made careful search and inquiry, seeking to know what person or time the Spirit...was indicating....It was revealed...that they were not serving themselves, but you, in these things which now have been announced to you through those who preached the gospel by the Holy Spirit" (1 Pet 1:10-12).

9 "Church," like "Israel," is a multi-faceted name/title, and one must know what is meant with its use: i.e., there is a "church system" that persecutes true Believers (Rev 3:16; 2 Tim 3:1-12; Matt 5:20), and a true *church*, an eternal *ekklesia*—which includes all who truly seek to follow the God of Israel (Acts 7:38; 2 Thes 1:1; 2:13). Also, there is a "Synagogue of Satan" that opposes Y'shua (John 8:44; 10:33; Rev 2:9; 3:9). In *Who Is Israel?* the word "church" is sometimes used to include those who, in this life, "*claim*" to belong to "the church." This same standard of including those who, in the end, the Father Himself may not include) also is applied in references to "Jews/Judaism." We trust that in the end, the Holy One Himself will decide who among both peoples is acceptable (Mat 7:23). Since the word "church" is often misunderstood, we prefer the Greek *ekklesia* (*Strong's* # G 1577) when referring to the *called out ones*. Also, the word "church" was possibly originally connected with the Latin *kirk* (circus). See *Smith's Bible Dictionary* by William Smith, L.L.D., Hendrickson,1998, *Church*, p 117.

10 According to the *Theological Wordbook...*, "Usually *kahal* is translated
(continued...)

ekklesia, [11] were one and the same. Just as our GOD is One, so in the end He will have but one called-out people. [12]

The Spirit of Adoption and Sons of Israel

Many people believe that only the non-Jews have to be adopted. However, *all*Believers must receive the "spirit of adoption" and by it become "sons of God." Receiving adoption empowers us to call the Almighty our Abba (Father). The fullness of our adoption is expressed in the redemption of our bodies. This spirit of adoption is specifically said to "belong to the sons of Israel," It likewise was given to the saints at Ephesus (perhaps they were scattered Israelites being re-gathered). The spirit of adoption is mentioned only five times in Scripture, and the verses never mention Abraham. They do not speak of non-Jewish Believers being adopted into Abraham's family. They speak of us becoming "born-again" sons of the Holy One:

---

10 (...continued)
ekklesia in the LXX [*Septuagint*]." See *TWOT* word # 1991a; page 790.
Septuagint: Greek translation of the Hebrew Old Covenant completed 200 years before Messiah's birth. Of the 122 KJV usages, more than 60 times *kahal* (*kehilat*) is translated *ekklesia* (*Hatch and Redpath Concordance to the Septuagint,* 1983, Baker, p 433); thirty-six times it is translated *synagogue,* as in Genesis 28:3 (*TWOT* word # 1991a). Like *ekklesia, kahal* and synagogue also describe an *assembly* (Strong's #'s H6951; G4864).
11 *Ekklesia* (εκκλησια), the New Covenant word translated *church* speaks of a "calling out," of a *meeting,* especially a religious *congregation,* an assembly (*Thayer's Greek-English Lexicon of the New Testament,* Baker, 1983, p 196a; *Strong's* # G 1577). In Acts 19:32 *ekklesia* is used to define the confused mob crying out against Paul. Thus, *assembly* might be a more appropriate translation.
12 One God, see Deu 6:4; Mark 12:29. One people, see Num 15:15; Ezek 37:19; John 17:11.

Paul tells those being led by the Spirit of God, "You have not received a spirit of slavery leading to fear again, but you have received a spirit of adoption as sons by which we cry out, "Abba! Father!" (Romans 8:15).

"The Spirit Himself testifies with our spirit that we are children of God" (Romans 8:16).

"And not only this, but also we ourselves, having the first fruits of the Spirit, even we ourselves groan within ourselves, waiting eagerly for our adoption as sons, the redemption of our body" (Romans 8:23).

Paul, speaks of his kinsmen according to the flesh, and says they "are Israelites, to whom belongs the adoption as sons, and the glory and the covenants and the giving of the Law and the temple service and the promises" (Romans 9:4).

Paul also says YHVH wanted to "redeem those who were under the Law, that we might receive the adoption as sons" (Galatians 4:5).

Paul wrote to the saints at Ephesus and told them that, YHVH "predestined us to adoption as sons through Messiah Y'shua to Himself, according to the kind intention of His will" (Ephesians 1:5).

The Olive Tree of Israel

Israel is first called an "olive tree" when Jeremiah spoke to "the house of Israel and the house of Judah," so we see there are two main branches in the tree. The first branches to be broken off were those of Israel (Ephraim). They were scattered among every nation where they became degenerate and wild. Then during the time of Y'shua many of Judah were broken off. In this tree Y'shua is the Root, the *life-source*. Even the patriarchs must have faith in and receive eternal life from Him.

"Israel is swallowed up; they are now among the nations like a vessel in which no one delights" (Hosea 8:8; also see Romans 9:21-24).

"I will shake the house of Israel among all nations as grain is shaken in a sieve, but not a kernel will fall to the ground [be lost to Me]" (Amos 9:9; see Hosea 5:3).

YHVH asks of Ephraim (who was taken captive to Assyria), "What are you doing...on the road to Assyria?" And, "I planted you a choice vine, a completely faithful seed. How then have you turned yourself before Me into the degenerate shoots of a foreign vine?" (Jeremiah 2:18,21). (For all outward purposes Ephraim became like degenerate foreigners, or pagan gentiles.)

When YHVH first called Israel an olive tree, Jeremiah said He was speaking to Ephraim and Judah. "The house of Israel and the house of Judah have broken My covenant, which I made with their fathers" (Jeremiah 11:10).

Jeremiah then said of both Israel and Judah, "YHVH called your name, 'A green olive tree, beautiful in fruit and form'" (Jeremiah 11:16).

King David said he was like a green olive tree, and that his children/seed were like olive plants. And Y'shua says, "I am the root and offspring/descendant of David, the bright morning star" (Psalms 52:8; 128:3; Revelation 22:16).

When the apostle Paul speaks of wild olive branches being "grafted into...the rich root of the olive tree," he is referring to the olive tree that had become denuded after Ephraim was scattered among the nations (Romans 11:17). So what is the mystery?

It is that whether Ephraim and Judah are natural or wild, both are olive branches, and Israel is the olive tree (Jeremiah 11:10,16; Romans 11:25).

Frequently Asked Questions

The following are brief excerpts taken from the "Frequently Asked Questions" (FAQ's) section of the messianicisrael.com web site.

Question: Do you believe *everyone* in the "Church" is an Ephraimite?

Answer: We follow our Messiah's example and answer a question with a question: Do those who inquire believe that *everyone* in "Judaism" is a biological descendant of Israel? Over the years have not the Jewish people made converts from among the Gentile Nations. Those who are asking this question generally call all Jewish people "Jews." In this same sense we call all Believers "*Ephraimites*."

Question: Are you saying that everyone has to be descended from Abraham to be saved?

Answer: Absolutely not. Genealogy cannot be proven for this many generations, as there are far too many genetic variables involved. This is true for Jew and non-Jew alike, because neither can prove, or disprove, a genetic connection to Abraham. However, much is being done to establish paternal genetics at this time. (See the book, *Who Is Israel?* for further elaboration on this point. Still, we do not encourage examination of family trees [1 Timothy 1:4]).

We well realize that our Father in Heaven has the right to add "others" to Israel. However, the questions we ask are: Do biologically unrelated followers fulfill the promise made to Abraham—that "myriads" of physical "seed" would come "from his own loins"? Further, could not some, perhaps the majority, of these "others" (these supposed Gentiles) in truth be descended from scattered Ephraim/Israel? (See Genesis 48:19; Romans 11:25.) In addition, since most of the "Early Church" were Jewish, many Believers could actually be descended from those early Jewish Believers. Over the years, many Jewish people had to hide from the persecution of the Church. Perhaps they escaped by hiding in the church. Moreover, regardless of what any of the above descendants believed, their biological grandfathers would still continue to be their grandfathers. On a physical basis, they would still continue to be "of Israel." Therefore, could it be that many of those being redeemed by the Messiah are in truth descendants of scattered Israel? (Hosea 1:10-11; 2:14-23; Ezekiel 34; John 10:11-14).

Is it reasonable to believe that early followers of the Messiah were cut off from being part of Israel because they lost touch with their Hebraic roots? These people had to choose between staying in the synagogues or following Messiah Y'shua. It opposes Scripture to say that those who followed Y'shua were cut off from Israel, whereas those who did not follow Him, but followed the Torah, were not cut off. (John 9:22; 12:42; 16:2; Acts 26:9-11; Romans 11:17,20).

All Israel was commanded to follow the "prophet like Moses." That Prophet is Y'shua. Could Believers be cut off for following Y'shua? This is not logical. (Deuteronomy 18:18-19; John 17:8,14-20; Mark 16:16; Acts 3:22-23; Hebrews 2:3; 3:2-7; 7:22; 10:26; 12:25).

Question: Do you believe that because someone is descended from the people of Ephraim (Israel), or for that matter, from Judah, that they are guaranteed "salvation"?

Answer: No, we absolutely do not. Israel is "chosen to choose" (Exodus 19:4-6; Deuteronomy 4:37; 7:6-8; 10:15; 28; 30:19). Moreover, Romans 9:6 tells us: "But it is not as though the word of God has failed. For they are not all Israel who are descended from Israel." Not everyone who is physically born of Israel is truly "of Israel." In Israel, descent from the patriarchs is not enough, one also must have faith. Esau well proves this point: Though descended from Isaac, only wrath from above is promised to uncaring Esau (Genesis 25:28-34; Hebrews 12:15-17; Malachi 1:2-4; Obadiah 1:6-9,17-18; Jeremiah 49:10).

Question: Do you agree with the idea of dividing Israel into "Spiritual and Physical" camps?

Answer: Y'shua said, "An hour is coming, and *now* is, when the true worshipers shall worship the Father in spirit and truth; for such people the Father seeks to be His worshipers" (John 4:23). *All Israel,* Jew and non-Jew alike, is called to worship YHVH "in spirit." Thus, to worship Him, "physical Israel" must be "spiritual." Further, every Believer in Messiah is a "physical being." Everyone descends from *someone.* The unspoken message of this theory is that the non-Jewish Believer does *not* descend from Abraham. Thus, this concept begs the question: *From whom do they descend?* This in turn calls for the twin answers that the patriarchs were promised myriads of biological heirs (Genesis 11:4; 15:5; 17:4; 26:4; 24:24, 60; 28:3, 14; 32:12; 48:4,16,19), and as to whom is of "physical"

Israel, only YHVH Himself can (and does) know (Hosea 5:3; 8:8; Amos 9:9; Deuteronomy 28:64).

Again, "Physical Israel" must be "spiritual" to please the Holy One. And *everyone* who claims to be "Spiritual Israel" is a "physical" being. Thus, there is a decided flaw in the idea of dividing Israel along these lines.

Question: What about unrelated "Believing Gentiles"? Are they too, part of Israel?

Answer: Yes they are. From the beginning, converts were to be regarded as "natives of the Land" (Exodus 12:48; Leviticus 19:34; Numbers 9:14; 15:15, 16; Deuteronomy 18:15-19; Ephesians 2:11-22).

Question: Do you believe in "Replacement Theology?

Answer: A true "parent" cannot "replace" one child with another, and neither would our Heavenly Father do such a thing. For this and other reasons, we oppose the idea that "the Church has replaced Israel." However, we also are against the present day claim by some that: now that the Jewish Believers are on the scene, YHVH is through with the non-Jewish, supposedly Gentile Believers. This appears to be a "Reverse Replacement Theology"—which is no more acceptable than is Christian "Replacement Theology." Both are destructive teachings.

We believe that every promise made to Judah will be absolutely fulfilled, even as will be fulfilled every promise made to Joseph/Ephraim. Neither house can be replaced.

For more Frequently Asked Questions, see FAQ's at,
messianicisrael.com

Prayer Points

Ephraim is especially called to be a "watchman" for the whole house of Israel (Hosea 9:8;Jer 30:24). He is called to cry out, "O YHVH, save Thy people the remnant of Israel" (Jer 31:7; Psa 5:3). We need watchmen who know that "the effective, fervent prayer of a righteous man availeth much" (James 5:16, KJV): *Effective:* he sees the problem. *Fervent:* he cares about solving it. *Righteous:* he is covered by Messiah's blood. Those who see the truth about "both the houses of Israel" need to pray for her full restoration.

- Pray that all whom the Father has chosen to "instruct" Ephraim in these latter-days would arise, that Ephraim might come to repentance and be "ashamed for the deeds of her youth" (Jer 31:18-19).
- Pray that Ephraim will cease to be "like a silly dove without sense" and that she will move beyond the "elementary things" and "press on to maturity" (Hos 7:11; Heb 6:1-17).
- Pray that all Israel will see the truth about the "melo hagoyim" promised to Ephraim, and that the "fullness of Gentiles" will come into its fullness, or maturity. Also pray that salvation through Y'shua will come to all Israel (Gen 48:19; Rom 11:25,26; Eph 4:15; Mat 1:21).

♦ Pray that YHVH will use the tragic events of our time to bring His people to repentance and faith in Him through the shed blood of Messiah Y'shua (Obad 1:12; Jer 5:12-14; Luke 13:1-5).

♦ Pray that those who are seeking answers will realize that the only true answers are found in the gospel, in the sacrificial Lamb, and in He Who paid the price for our sins (1 Cor 7:23; Mat 27:9).

♦ Pray that wisdom and discernment will be granted to those who have been granted influence over Israel in spiritual, political and financial arenas (Dan 2:21; 4:32; 5:21; Rom 13:1).

♦ Pray that the sheep of Israel will be delivered from the wicked shepherds who muddy the waters and feed themselves rather than the flock. Pray that the sheep will be snatched out of the hands of these wicked shepherds. Pray that all wolves in sheep's clothing and all false prophets will be exposed for who they are in truth (Ezek 34; Jer 23:1-3; Mat 7:15).

♦ Pray that Ephraim will cease to be jealous of Judah, regardless of whether that jealousy is acted out in violence, or in simply wishing they were Jewish. Pray that Ephraim will judge with righteous judgment, and that in their desire to be reunited with Judah they will not trade errant Christian ways for errant Jewish ways (Isa 11:13; Jer 31:21-25; John 7:24).

♦ Pray that the hearts of Ephraim and Judah might be circumcised with a love for one another, pray that each will learn to give credit where it is due, and that each will objectively see the role they have played as part of the people of Israel: Ephraim in declaring salvation through Messiah, and Judah in declaring the truths of Torah (Gen 48:19; 2 Chr 11:4; Ezek 37:15-28).

♦ Pray that Ephraim fulfill his divine mandate, which is to walk in a way that honors Torah and thus provokes Judah to want what he has. Pray that Ephraim will make Judah jealous rather than being jealous of Judah, which causes him to lose his effectiveness (Rom 9:25,26; 10:19; 11:11; Hos 1:9,0; 2:23).

♦ Pray that the veil will be lifted from the eyes of both the houses of Israel so they will see the truth of Y'shua and cease to stumble over Him (Isa 8:14; Rom 11:25; John 2:22).

♦ Pray that both houses quickly understand YHVH's plan to have a sinless, overcoming army, and that they give themselves fully to becoming that great army (Isa 11:11-14; 27:6-9; Zech 8:3,7,13; 9:13; 10:7-10; Hos 11:10; Obad 1:18; Jer 50:4,5,20; 3:14-18; Ezek 37:22-26).

♦ Pray that Ephraim would "be like a mighty man, with their heart glad as if from wine," and that "their children see it and be glad" and that "their heart rejoice in YHVH" (Zec 10:7).

♦ Pray that the "Standard," Y'shua, will be lifted up in all His glory and that the world will see Him in truth, and not according to manmade religion (Isa 11:12).

♦ "Pray for the peace of Jerusalem, and that they who love her would prosper; that peace be within her walls and prosperity within her palaces" (Psa 122:6,7).

- Pray for Jerusalem to become the City of Truth, and to acknowledge Messiah Y'shua as her "King of Kings" (Psa 48:2; Zec 8:3; Mat 5:35; 23:37-39; Rev 17:14; 19:16).
- Pray for the safety and well-being of those of Judah who have returned to the Promised Land; pray their hearts will be turned toward their fathers and that angels will be given charge over them (Isa 11:11; Luke 1:17; Psa 91:11).
- Pray that even as YHVH has gathered for a "second time" the "dispersed of Judah," He will "restore their fortunes," and enter into judgment with those who "harass" her (Isa 11:11-13; Joel 3:1-2).
- Pray that "the sons of Israel come, both they and the sons of Judah" and that they "go along weeping" in a true search for their God; pray they turn their faces toward Zion and truly be joined in covenant with Him (Jer 50:4-5).
- Pray that Israel will seek to pay the full price for their pardon, and that all their pagan practices and idols will be made like "chalk stones," and so will be unable to stand (Isa 27:9).
- Pray that Israel's mighty ones will be equipped with the breath of the Spirit of the Most High (Ezekiel 37:10).
- Pray that the sons of Israel who are pursuing this work of the Kingdom will be strong and courageous; pray that the spirit of Joshua and Caleb will be upon them, and that they know that, in the strength of the Holy One they can go in and take the Land (Joshua 1:6-9,18; 10:25). *Amen! So be it!*

Maps And Charts

The Different Dispersions And Times of Ephraim and Judah

| | Different Dispersions | → Ephraim 721-722 B.C. |
| | | ⋯⋯ Judah 586 B.C. |

To understand Israel, we must see that
Ephraim and Judah were dispersed at different times,
and that they were sent to different locations. There was
more than 135 years between the times of their
dispersions, and as much as 500 miles difference in the
locations to which they were dispersed.

-35-

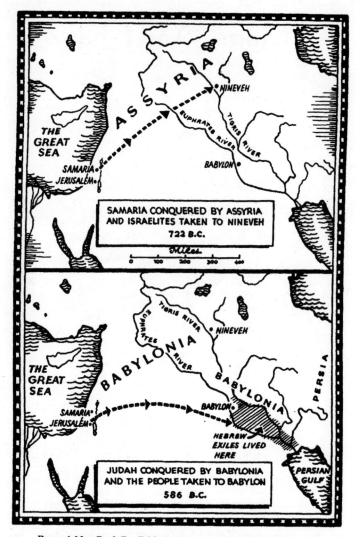

From *A Map Book For Bible Students* by Frederick L. Fay, pg 18,
Old Tappan, NJ: Fleming H. Revell. Used by permission.

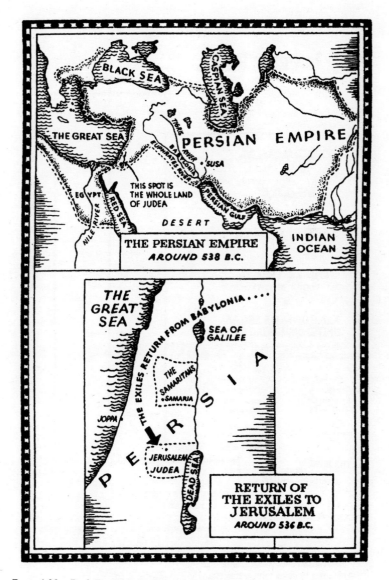

THE PERSIAN EMPIRE
AROUND 538 B.C.

RETURN OF
THE EXILES TO
JERUSALEM
AROUND 536 B.C.

From *A Map Book For Bible Students* by Frederick L. Fay, pg 20, Old Tappan, NJ:
Fleming H. Revell. Used by permission.

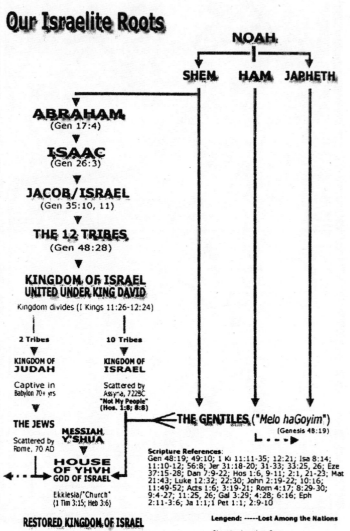

Our Israelite Roots

NOAH

SHEM · HAM · JAPHETH

ABRAHAM
(Gen 17:4)

ISAAC
(Gen 26:3)

JACOB/ISRAEL
(Gen 35:10, 11)

THE 12 TRIBES
(Gen 48:28)

KINGDOM OF ISRAEL
UNITED UNDER KING DAVID

Kingdom divides (1 Kings 11:26-12:24)

2 Tribes

KINGDOM OF
JUDAH

Captive in
Babylon 70+ yrs

THE JEWS

Scattered by
Rome, 70 AD

10 Tribes

KINGDOM OF
ISRAEL

Scattered by
Assyria, 722BC
"Not My People"
(Hos. 1:8; 8:8)

THE GENTILES ("Melo haGoyim")
(Genesis 48:19)

MESSIAH
Y'SHUA

HOUSE
OF YHVH
GOD OF ISRAEL

Ekklesia/"Church"
(1 Tim 3:15; Heb 3:6)

Scripture References:
Gen 48:19; 49:10; 1 Ki 11:11-35; 12:21; Isa 8:14;
11:10-12; 56:8; Jer 31:18-20; 31-33; 33:25, 26; Eze
37:15-28; Dan 7:9-22; Hos 1:6, 9-11; 2:1, 21-23; Mat
21:43; Luke 12:32; 22:30; John 2:19-22; 10:16;
11:49-52; Acts 1:6; 3:19-21; Rom 4:17; 8:29-30;
9:4-27; 11:25, 26; Gal 3:29; 4:28; 6:16; Eph
2:11-3:6; Ja 1:1;1 Pet 1:1; 2:9-10

RESTORED KINGDOM OF ISRAEL
UNITED UNDER THE SON OF DAVID, MESSIAH Y'SHUA

Lengend: -----Lost Among the Nations

Chart by Jonathan Sexton
© 2002, *Who Is Israel?* by Batya Wootten

There Are Two Main Branches In The Olive Tree of Israel: Ephraim and Judah

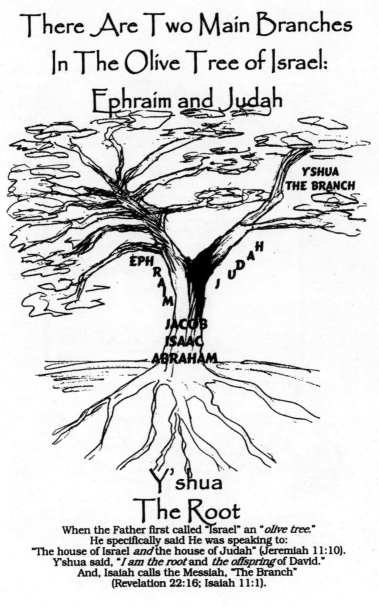

Y'shua The Root

When the Father first called "Israel" an "*olive tree.*"
He specifically said He was speaking to:
"The house of Israel *and* the house of Judah" (Jeremiah 11:10).
Y'shua said, "*I am the root* and *the offspring* of David."
And, Isaiah calls the Messiah, "The Branch"
(Revelation 22:16; Isaiah 11:1).

Ephraim and Judah   Israel Revealed

The Fall and Restoration of Israel's Kingdom

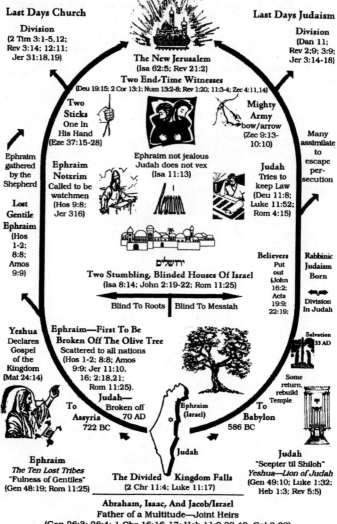

Last Days Church
Division
(2 Tim 3:1-5,12;
Rev 3:14; 12:11;
Jer 31:18,19)

Last Days Judaism
Division
(Dan 11;
Rev 2;9; 3:9;
Jer 3:14-18)

The New Jerusalem
(Isa 62:5; Rev 21:2)
Two End-Time Witnesses
(Deu 19:15; 2 Cor 13:1; Num 13:2-8; Rev 1:20; 11:3-4; Zec 4:11,14)

Two
Sticks
One In
His Hand
(Eze 37:15-28)

Mighty
Army
bow/arrow
(Zec 9:13-
10:10)

Many
assimilate
to
escape
per-
secution

Ephraim
gathered
by the
Shepherd

Ephraim
Notzrim
Called to be
watchmen
(Hos 9:8;
Jer 316)

Ephraim not jealous
Judah does not vex
(Isa 11:13)

Judah
Tries to
keep Law
(Deu 11:8;
Luke 11:52;
Rom 4:15)

Lost
Gentile
Ephraim
(Hos
1-2;
8:8;
Amos
9:9)

ירושלים
Two Stumbling, Blinded Houses Of Israel
(Isa 8:14; John 2:19-22; Rom 11:25)

Blind To Roots   Blind To Messiah

Believers
Put
out
(John
16:2;
Acts
19:9;
22:19;

Rabbinic
Judaism
Born

Division
In Judah

Yeshua
Declares
Gospel
of the
Kingdom
(Mat 24:14)

Ephraim—First To Be
Broken Off The Olive Tree
Scattered to all nations
(Hos 1-2; 8:8; Amos
9:9; Jer 11:10,
16; 2:18,21;
Rom 11:25).
Judah—
Broken off
70 AD

Salvation
33 AD

Some
return,
rebuild
Temple

To
Assyria
722 BC

Ephraim
(Israel)

To
Babylon
586 BC

Judah

Ephraim
The Ten Lost Tribes
"Fulness of Gentiles"
(Gen 48:19; Rom 11:25)

The Divided   Kingdom Falls
(2 Chr 11:4; Luke 11:17)

Judah
"Scepter til Shiloh"
Yeshua—Lion of Judah
(Gen 49:10; Luke 1:32;
Heb 1:3; Rev 5:5)

Abraham, Isaac, And Jacob/Israel
Father of a Multitude—Joint Heirs
(Gen 26:3; 28:4; 1 Chr 16:16-17; Heb 11:9,39,40; Gal 3:29)

The Hope of Messianic Israel

Messianic Israel believes *Y'shua Ha'Natsree* (Jesus of Nazareth) was and is the true Messiah, the Lion of Judah, the Branch Who will fully reunite all Israel; that He died and rose from the dead and lives at the right hand of the Almighty; and according to the ancient Holy Scriptures, Y'shua is YHVH Elohim appearing in the flesh, as Y'shua demonstrated in Himself (Deu 18:18-19; John 8:58; 10:33; Mat 12:6-8; 9:35; 15:31; Isa 11; 53; Micah 5:2-4; Luke 24:46; Isa 8:14; John 2:22; Acts 3:15-17; Heb 13:20; 1 John 4:2; 2 John 1:7; Rev 5:5; John 1:1).

Messianic Israel believes we are made righteous in Messiah Y'shua. (He is the heart of Abraham's unconditional covenant.) The sign of the New Covenant is circumcision of the heart, which leads to confession, salvation, faith, grace, and to good works in Messiah. The conditional Mosaic covenant presents the eternal truths of Torah (YHVH's teaching and instructions) to His people, the hearing of which brings about blessing or curse (respond and be blessed, disobey and lack). In the New Covenant, Y'shua's Law is to be written on our hearts by the Spirit (Rom 4:13-16; 5:2; 10:10; 1 Pet 1:19; 2 Cor 5:21; Gal 3:16,29; Titus 3:5; Heb 10:38; 1 John 1:9; Eph 2:8; James 2:14; Deu 28; Ezek 36:26; Jer 31:31-33; Heb 10:16; Gal 2:16; John 5:46; 10;30; 14:2; 15:10).

Messianic Israel is a people whose heart's desire is to fully reunite the olive tree of Israel—both branches —Ephraim and Judah—into one, redeemed, nation of Israel—through Messiah Y'shua. They seek to arouse Ephraim from obscurity, and by example, to awaken Judah to the Messiah—and thus to hasten both Y'shua's return to Earth and the restoration of the promised Kingdom to Israel (Mat 6:10; 12:25; 21:43; 24:43; Luke 22:29-30; Mark 13:34; Luke 22:29-30; 2 Chr 11:4; Eze 37:15-28; Jer 11:10,16; 2:18,21; Rom 11:17,24; Eph 2:11-22; Acts 1:6).

Messianic Israel deems the Jewish people to be the identifiable representatives and offspring of Judah and "the children of Israel, his companions," and that non-Jewish followers of the Messiah from all nations have been, up to now, the unidentifiable representatives and offspring of Ephraim and "all the house of Israel, his companions" (Gen 48:19; Hosea 1-2; 5:3; Eze 37:16; Jer 31:6-9; Gen 15:2-5; 26:3; 28:4; Heb 11:9; Isa 56:3,6-8; Eph 2:11-22).

Messianic Israel affirms that the Jewish people have been kept identifiable as seed of the patriarch Jacob, YHVH's covenant people, to preserve His Holy Torah (Law), Feasts, and Shabbat (Sabbath); that the salvation of the Jewish people through their acceptance of Messiah Y'shua, will be the crowning act of mankind's redemption, and is necessary for the restoration of the Kingdom to Israel. Further, the Father plans that Ephraim, they being the "wild olive branch," stimulate Judah to want what they have; they are called to walk in a way that will make Judah jealous of their relationship with the God of Israel (Gen

48:19; Isa 11:13; 37:31,32; Zec 2:12; Eze 37:15-28; Hosea 1:7; Rom 10:19; 11:11,14; Mat 23:39).

Messianic Israel believes the non-Jewish followers of Y'shua are predominantly returning Ephraim, those who were once among the Gentiles/Goyim/Nations as "*LoAmi*,"or "Not a people," but have now been restored to the commonwealth of Israel through their covenant with Israel's Messiah; that, they are no more Gentiles/ Goyim/of the Nations, but fulfill the promised restoration of uprooted Ephraim, and Jacob's prophecy that Ephraim would become "*melo hagoyim*," the "*fullness of the Gentiles/Goyim/Nations.*" As Ephraim, they have been kept in mystery until recently, being used to preserve the testimony of Y'shua, the Messiah of all Israel.   Their awakening, recognition, and performance as Ephraim, and their union with Judah, is a necessity for salvation of "all" Israel, and the restoration of the Kingdom to Israel (Gen 48:19; Hosea 1:9-10; 5:3; 8:8; Amos 9:9; Jer 31:18-19; Zec 10:7; Rom 9:24-26; 11:26; Eph 2:11-22).

Messianic Israel declares that Believers in Y'shua were not meant to replace Judah as Israel, but as "Ephraim," they are part of the called out ones (*ekklesia*), and in these latter-days, the Father is leading them to, whenever Scripturally possible, join with Judah; that Judah (faithful Jewish ones who will receive Messiah) and Ephraim (faithful non-Jewish Messiah followers) ultimately will fulfill the destiny of the two houses of Israel: that together they might fulfill the prophesies about the one, unified, victorious people of Israel (Jer 31:9; Rom 8:29; Col 1:15,18; 2:12; Heb 12:22-24; Lev 23:2-36; Exo 19:5; 1 Pet 1:1; 2:9;

Ephraim and Judah Israel Revealed

Jer 3:18; 23:6; Zec 8:13; 12:1-5; Mat 25:31-46; Exo 12:48-49; Num 15:15-16; Isa 56:3,6-8).

Messianic Israel maintains that up to this general time "blindness in part" has happened to all (both houses) of Israel, and as the blinders are lifted, non-Jewish followers in Y'shua will gain insight into their role as Ephraim and become defenders of Scriptural Torah and of Judah, and due to this character change, many Jewish people will accept Y'shua as Messiah. This process has begun as indicated through the Messianic Jewish movement (Judah), the Christian Zionism movement (Ephraim), and the Messianic Israel movement (union of Judah and Ephraim) (Isa 8:14; 11:13; Rom 11:25,26; Jer 33:14-16; 31:18-19; Ezek 37:15-28).

The reunion and full restoration of the two houses:
This is the hope that burns in the hearts of those of Messianic Israel...

© 1996-2002
Messianic Israel Ministries
PO Box 700217, Saint Cloud, FL 34770
www.mim.net

Want More?

Visit the Messianic Israel Alliance Web Page
www.messianicisrael.com
Read the Inspiring Articles Found There
Check out Our Local Fellowship Listings
Join Our Email List for Enlightening Bulletins
Subscribe to Our Magazine:
The Messianic Israel Herald

Batya Ruth Wootten

In 1977, Batya Wootten operated a bookstore/catalogue company that was primarily funded by her husband, Angus. The store needed someone to fund it because it specialized in materials and books about Israel, the Jewish people, Christians, and how they all relate. At the time, interest in the subject matter was marginal at best. Some even reacted to it with hostility.

Because she felt a responsibility to know what the books they were offering said, and so that she might write catalog descriptions for them, she read countless books about the subject of Israel.

Much to her dismay, she discovered a wide variety of opinion about Israel's true role in the world, its future, and most important, about Israel's identity. She felt stymied.

Batya and Angus had endless discussions about "Israel." Then, being in spiritual anguish over the matter Batya began to cry out in earnest to her Heavenly Father, asking Him for *His* answer to her ever-present question, "*Who Is Israel?*"

Even as He promises to answer us, so the GOD of Israel answered her. He began to open up the Scriptures to her and satisfied her heart-cry, which led to her first book, *In Search of Israel*, and then to *The Olive Tree of Israel*. Next, she wrote the comprehensive book, "*Who Is Israel?*" (1998, 2000) and its companion *Study Guide* (2001). Then came the book you now hold in your hand, *Ephraim and Judah Israel Revealed*.

Batya's books represent decades of study, discussion, prayer, and meditation on this crucial issue. Readers will come away changed for eternal good by the revelations and insights contained within them. Surely, they will help to restore a brotherhood broken long ago.

Batya also is the author of the forthcoming book, *Israel's Feasts and Their Fullness* (Spring, 2002). She is married to her best friend, Col. Angus Wootten (Ret.), author of the visionary book, *Restoring Israel's Kingdom*.

Together, Angus and Batya have ten children who have blessed them with many grandchildren and great-grandchildren. Working hand in glove, Angus and Batya pioneered the House of David Catalogue (a first of its kind). This "profit-less business" soon became an official "non-profit (5013(c) ministry)" (in 1982). This change, not only in status but also in focus, led to their publishing the enlightening monthly Newsletter, the *House of David Herald*, which ultimately became a Magazine, *The Messianic Israel Herald*. They also developed the informative Messianic Israel web site: www.mim.net—and—messianicisrael.com—which in turn led to the founding of the *Messianic Israel Alliance*—a rapidly growing Alliance of congregations, synagogues, and home fellowships that agree with *The Hope of Messianic Israel*. This cutting-edge Alliance is served by a dedicated Shepherds Council.

Angus and Batya's efforts have served—and continue to help serve—to develop greater understanding of, and fresh insight into, the GOD of Israel and His chosen people.

Read their writings and be blessed.

"Let the one who is taught share all good things with him who teaches" (Galatians 6:6).
If through this book a good thing has been accomplished in your life, please write and share your good news with me. Write to:

Batya Wootten

PO Box 700217, Saint Cloud, FL 34770

e-mail: batya@mim.net

—Who Is— Israel?
Enlarged Edition
by Batya Wootten

This phenomenal book is causing a stir—because it clarifies misunderstandings about Israel. The truth about "both the houses of Israel" (Isaiah 8:14) is causing a reformation in the Body of Messiah! Read this solution driven book and see the truth that is inspiring Believers everywhere!

Who is Israel? Why do *you* even need to know? Because knowing who you are and where you are going is vital to your relationship with the GOD of Israel.

You need to read this book because it will: Inspire and encourage you, even change your life — Help you discover your own Hebraic Heritage — Put your feet on the road to Zion. Read this Scriptural account of Israel and understand: Israel, the Church, the Bible — The mystery of the "fullness of the Gentiles" — The "blindness of 'Israel'" — The Father's master plan for Israel — This guidebook will explain why you: Feel something is "missing" in your life — Have an unexplainable love for Israel and Jewish people — Feel an urge to celebrate the feasts of Israel.

This handbook will help you to: Move from religion to relationship — Unmuddle the muddled doctrines of Christianity — Properly intercede for "all Israel" — Remove the stones from Israel's road home — Live the *Shema*, the heart of New Covenant faith — Fulfill the latter-day desires of the Father's heart. The Biblical truths unveiled in this volume will help: Put an end to "Christian" anti-Semitism — Heal divisions in the Body of Messiah — Cure the plague of "Believer's Boredom" — Relieve "rootlessness" in non-Jews who love "Israel." This book: Leads us back to our First Love — Lifts up Messiah Y'shua — Gives Him His proper place — Shows how He is the epitome of all that is "Israel." The revelation that unfolds on these pages will enrich your relationship with the Holy One of Israel; it will lead Jewish and non-Jewish Believers (Judah and Ephraim) to become the promised "one new man." Read them and be blessed.

This enlightening book includes a Foreword and Introduction, plus the following encouraging chapters: Believing What Abraham Believed — Israel: A Blessing — Jacob's Firstborn Heir — Ephraim: A Profile — Yankees and Rebels — LoAmmi: Not A People — Many Israels, One Israel — A Priceless Gift — Chosen To Choose — The Blood, The Redeemer, And Physical Israel — Literal or Spiritual? — Israel: A Mystery Until — "Holey" Doctrines — More Tattered Theories — Is Judah All Israel? — Leaving Elementary Things Behind — From Orphans To Heirs — The Olive Tree of Israel — One Law, One People — The Two Witnesses And Their Fullness — Called to Be Watchmen — Return, O Virgin Israel! — Y'shua: Epitome of All That Is Israel — An Israel Yet To Come. This Enlarged Edition includes, Maps and Charts — Israel In Progress — Index — Bibliography — Informative Addendum about current Jewish genetic research. ISBN 1-886987-03-3 Paper, 304 pages $14.95.

Also Available in Spanish!

¿Quién es Israel?

Por Batya Wootten
Traducido al Español por Natalie Pavlik
ISBN 1-886987-08-4 $14.95

Who Is Israel?
Now Available as A Study Guide

Who Is Israel? and its companion
Study Guide are causing a phenomenal
stir among Bible Believers! The truth
about "both the houses of Israel" (Isaiah
8:14) is causing a reformation in the
Body of Messiah! Read the book, study
the Guide, and find out what is inspiring
so many Believers in this last day!

This Guide can be used as a twelve or twenty-four week
Study Course. (Completion Certificates available with
quantity orders). The Study Plan is simple: Gather a group
of people who will agree to meet for a specified time, one that
has an end in sight and a specific goal in mind, such as
understanding Israel and their part in Israel. Read and
discuss the listed Scriptures with your family and friends.
Propose a prior reading of the corresponding chapter(s) in
Who Is Israel? during the week. Sample Questions are listed
in the Study Guide, with Answers in the back. We suggest
each person read a section in the Lesson (mostly Scriptures),
rotating around the room until completed. Then ask the
questions. Reading and discussing the selected texts among
brethren builds up your faith and makes Scripture come
alive with new meaning. This plan calls for minimal
preparation on the part of the leader.

If you want fellowship with Believers of like mind, order
a case of these Study Guides and get started today!

ISBN 1-886987-08-4, Paper, 288 pages, $12.95
Case of Ten: $85.00 (plus shipping)

Please add appropriate Shipping To all Orders

Israel's Feasts
And Their
Fullness

by
Batya Wootten

Israel's Feasts And Their Fullness *by Batya Wootten* As Believers in the Messiah, how do we celebrate the feasts? Do we simply follow the traditions of our Jewish brothers, or is there something more we need to see about Israel's appointed times? To answer, we need to ask ourselves *why* we celebrate. Once we understand *why* so many non-Jewish Believers now feel called to honor the feasts, our answer will show us *how* to celebrate. The answer to "why" will inspire us as to "how." Understanding why we celebrate will also encourage us and help us to recognize why we feel as we do, and will add a rewarding sense of purpose to our celebrations. This inspiring book addresses the feasts for the people of Messianic Israel and offers suggestions for celebration—whether you are alone or with great numbers. It also presents these truths in light of our faith in Messiah Y'shua and in light of the role we are to play in bringing restoration to all Israel. Chapters Include: Who Is Celebrating and Why —The Return of The Prodigal, The Purpose of Celebration — Shabbat, Burden or Blessing — Havdallah, The First New Covenant Meeting? — New Moons — Celebrating The Four Passovers — Unleavened Bread — The First of First Fruits and the Resurrection — Shavuot and Two Unleavened Loaves —Yom Teruah and The Twin Silver Trumpets — Yom Kippur and You — Tabernacles and Y'shua — Tabernacles and The Great Day. Also includes Celebration Instruction pages for Shabbat, Havdallah and Passover. (Available Spring, '02.) ISBN 1-886987-02-5, Paper 384 pages $16.95

All Book Prices Are Plus Shipping—Tripled for Overseas

RESTORING ISRAEL'S
KINGDOM

by Angus Wootten

What was the last question Messiah Y'shua's disciples asked their Teacher as they stood on the Mount of Olives, knowing that He was about to depart? What mattered most to them?

As followers of Israel's Messiah, have we asked the question that mattered so much to His chosen twelve? With olive groves serving as a backdrop, these fathers of our faith asked the King of Israel, "Lord, is it at this time You are restoring the kingdom to Israel?" (Acts 1:6).

Why did Y'shua's disciples, who had been trained by Him for more than three years, ask this particular question? Could it be because He had taught them to pray to our Father in Heaven, "Thy Kingdom come, on earth, as it is in Heaven"? (Matthew 6:10).

Since we are a people dedicated to bringing Y'shua's Kingdom to this earth, we must not lose sight of the vision that burned in the hearts of His first disciples. As part of His "chosen people" (1 Peter 1:1; 2:9), we must not lose sight of what should be our ultimate goal.

But, have we forgotten this important goal, even as we have lost sight or our heritage as part Israel? Could we be part of Ephraim/Israel—those so long ago blinded to the truth of their Israelite roots? (Genesis 48:19; Hosea 1-2; 8:8; Amos 9:9).

Just as Judah is beginning to see the Messiah, is the veil likewise being lifted from our "partially blinded" Israelite eyes? Do we belong to Israel's "olive tree" in a greater way than we had previously imagined? (Isaiah 8:14; Romans

-51-

11:25; Jeremiah 31:18-19; 11:10,16; 2:18,21). Is that why we are feeling a longing in our hearts for something more? Do we now feel a hunger deep within because the "set time" to restore Israel's Kingdom is upon us? If so, are we prepared to work toward that goal?

Restoring Israel's Kingdom offers the following challenging chapters: Are You Prepared? — Can We Make A Difference — Learning the Lessons of History — A Brief History of Israel — Lessons Learned — The Voice of The People — Who Told You? — Who Is A Jew? A Look At Israel's Bloodline — Our Hope of Glory And The Mystery of The Gentiles — The Way of The Gentiles — Ephraim, Once Again A Mighty Man — Ephraim Should Know More About Judah — From Roman Roads To The World Wide Web — The Jubilee Generation — A Mandate For Ephraim — Restoring The Kingdom To Israel — The Messianic Vision — When Will Y'shua Return — Preparing For The Final Battle. Plus a helpful Index.

Don't miss this exciting book! It will help you keep your eye on the goal, which is, the restoration of the Kingdom to the restored house of Israel.

ISBN 1-886987-04-1, Paper, 304 pages, $14.95 plus shipping

Another Great Book From Key of David Publishing

unlocking your future...

Distributed by—

MESSIANIC ISRAEL MINISTRIES

Write or Call For a FREE Catalog!!:
PO Box 700217, Saint Cloud, FL 34770
1 800 829-8777

Take Two Tablets Daily
The 10 Commandments and 613 Laws
by Angus Wootten

The 10 Commandments
and the 613 Laws

Angus Wootten

"You're trying to put me under the Law!"

This cry is often heard from Christians when they are presented with the laws and commandments of the God of Abraham, Isaac and Jacob.

Is their cry justified?

This invaluable book will help you to thoughtfully examine the laws the Holy One gave to His people through Moses. Read it and see that the Father's commandments were given for the physical and spiritual guidance of His people. His judgments and precepts were given, not to punish Israel, but to guide them, both as individuals and as a nation. They were given to help them become strong, courageous, healthy and blessed remnants of the Most High.

A handy guide, this work conveniently lists the 613 laws, divided into Mandatory Commandments and Prohibitions (according to Jewish custom), plus the Scripture verse(s) from which each law is derived.

Chapter titles include: Under the Law? — Y'shua's Attitude Toward the Law — Our Need For Law And Order — YHVH's Law or Man's Law? — Paul and the Law — Principles of the Protestant Reformation — What Should Be Our Attitude Toward the Law? — The Decalogue: The Ten Commandments.

YHVH's Word is like medicinal ointment, and nothing is more symbolic of His Word than the two tablets on which He wrote His desires for us. Taken daily, these "Two Tablets" will give us life more abundantly. This reference book should be in every Believers library. It is a must read!

ISBN1-886987-06-8   96 Informative pages, $4.95

EPHRAIM IN DEED *The Lost Tribes and Their Fulfillment of Prophecy* by John Hulley Does the Bible foretell what the Ephraimites should be doing today? If so, to identify them, we have only to look for the people who are fulfilling those prophecies. Decades of research by Harvard- educated John Hulley have resulted in a convincing account of Ephraimite activities from the Assyrian exile down to our time. Shows their role in the continuing battle for the restoration of Israel and reveals what they will be doing next. (Summer '02)
ISBN 1-886987-10-6,   320 Pages, $16.95

Ephraim Who? by *Jill Chamberlain Hulley.* This 10-week Bible study has helped many Believers find a biblical basis for what they have sensed to be true: they are part of Ephraim. Ideal for group or individual study, the book takes you from the tribes beginning in Genesis to their glorious end in Revelation. Reinforcing the biblical truth are findings from John Hulley's research into the tribes' itinerary and subsequent history. Compelling evidence of how they are fulfilling their prophetic destiny.
ISBN 1-886987-13-0,   36 Pages, 8 1/2 x 11 size, $8.00

Ephraim In Sixty Minutes by *Jill Chamberlain Hulley* Ever wondered where the lost tribes went, who they are? What's the point of finding them? This booklet provides answers. Ideal for those new to the subject, it is an appetizer for *Ephraim Who?* An in depth Bible study into the two House truth, this book features some of the findings from John Hulley's forthcoming book—which shows how the tribes are fulfilling their prophetic destiny in history and across continents. ISBN 1-886987-12-2 96 Pages, $15.00

MORE LIFE CHANGING BOOKS

My Beloved's Israel by Gloria Cavallaro
Deepen your personal relationship with your Bridegroom. Embark on an intimate journey into the heart of our Heavenly Father. Experience relationship with the Holy One of Israel like David described in his Psalms. Know intimacy with the Bridegroom like Solomon spoke of in his Song of Songs. A spirit-filled Believer, Gloria chronicles her visions and dreams, then interprets/journals them in light of Scriptural reflection. Israel must be reunited if they are to be prepared for coming latter-day challenges. This journal exhorts and encourages intimacy with the Holy One. It helps prepare ones heart. ISBN 1-886987-05-X 384 pages, $16.95.

ALL ISRAEL DANCES TOWARD THE TABERNACLE *by Chester Anderson and Tina Clemens* This inspiring book will help you understand the dynamics of worship. It takes you beyond the pale of other worship books and answers your many dance related questions. For example, What is dance? — How did it originate? — What if I don't know how to dance? — Does something special happen in the Heavenlies when we dance? — What attitude should be in our hearts

when we are dancing and why? — Why do I feel so drawn to Hebraic dance? — Why has Davidic dance become so popular? — How does dance come into play in the restoration of both the houses of Israel? This book will fill your heart with hope for the Glory that is soon to be upon us! It will set your feet a dancin'.

ISBN 1-886987-09-2 Paper, 192 pages. $12.95 plus shipping.

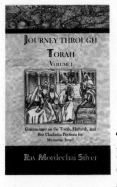

Journey Through Torah Volume I: Commentary on the Torah, Haftarah and Brit Chadoshah Portions for Messianic Israel
by Rav Mordechai Silver

Rav Silver offers Fifty-Two encouraging Torah teachings especially for Messianic Israel—all based on the Jewish tradition of reading certain "portions" of the Torah and the Prophets each week. Comments are founded on the truth that Yahweh is presently reuniting the two sticks of Judah and Ephraim. Silver, a Jewish Believer in the Messiah, repeatedly reaffirms that reunion. Corroborating teachings from the Brit Chadoshah (New Covenant) are included, plus a calendar/ listing which lists each of the portions. Inspiring regular readings for those seeking to return to their Hebraic roots. Those who long for Israel's full restoration won't want to miss these enlightening teachings. (Spring '02)

ISBN 1-886987-10-6,   288 pages $14.95

Want More Great Torah Teachings?

Want more teachings from both the
Old and New Covenants?

Register at our web site to receive weekly email Torah Commentaries and teachings from Rav Silver and other Messianic Israel leaders and teachers.

Go to Registrations at <messianicisrael.com>.

Torah Commentaries are posted in the *TorahScope* section of our web site. Go to *TorahScope*, then to Messianic Israel's Torah Commentaries, at:

messianicisrael.com

Ephraim and Judah
Israel Revealed
by Batya Wootten
Forward by Angus Wootten

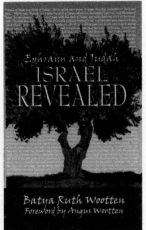

This brief book offers a succinct and updated overview of the material presented in the best-selling seminal classic, *Who Is Israel?*, by Batya Wootten. It includes maps, charts, and lists that clarify misconceptions about Israel's Twelve Tribes. Like Batya's other solution driven writings, this book is sure to cause a phenomenal stir among Believers. The truth about both houses of Israel is encouraging a reformation in the Body of Messiah. Read this Scripture-based book and find out what is inspiring Believers in these end-times!

This excellent tool will help those of non-Jewish Israel to come to know themselves, to see that they too are part of Israel (Jeremiah 31:18-19). It will help all Israel, both houses (Isaiah 8:14), to readily see how and where they fit into the Father's Divine plan. It will even help bring about the restoration of the Kingdom to the whole House of Israel.

Ephraim and Judah: Israel Revealed—Inexpensive, succinct and easy-to-read, it readily outlines the essence of Messianic Israel teachings.

ISBN 1-886987-11-4
Paper, 80 pages, $ 3.95 plus shipping

Quantity Discounts Available:
Call Messianic Israel Ministries
800 829 8777

Ephraim and Judah   Israel Revealed

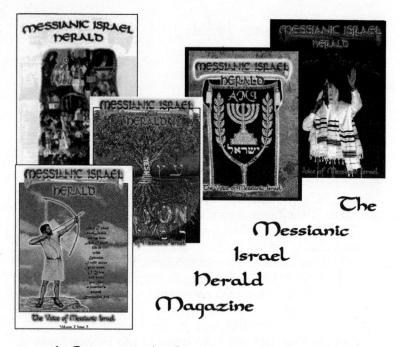

The
Messianic
Israel
Herald
Magazine

Informative! Challenging!! Inspiring!!!
Published Quarterly. Stay Informed! Subscribe
Today! $24.00 per Year (Back Issues Available)
Visit Us At Our Cutting Edge Website

Messianic Israel Ministries

www.mim.net